ACROSS
TWO
WORLDS

ACROSS TWO WORLDS

Selected Prose of

EGHISHÉ CHARENTS

Letters, excerpts from "Erkir Nayiri"
and "Erevan's House of Correction," essays,
and pages from his diary, translated by
Jack Antreassian and Marzbed Margossian,
with introduction and notes by the latter.

Ashod Press, New York, 1985

All the material in this book, including most of the annotations, have been translated from *The Collected Works* of Eghishe Charents, published by the Armenian Academy of Sciences between 1962 and 1967 in a six-volume set, edited by S. Aghababian, A. Zakarian, E. Topjian, A. Injikian, and K. Mahari. In 1983 a seventh volume appeared, containing most of Charents' unpublished works; it was prepared and annotated by the poet's daughter, Anahid Charents.

FIRST EDITION

Library of Congress Cataloging-in-Publication Data
Ch'arents', Eghishe, 1897-1937.
Across two worlds.
I. Title.
PK8548.C5A26   1985   891'.9928508   85-18625
ISBN 0-935102-17-5

Contents

Introduction

It is not our intention to diminish any of our post-holocaust writers when we identify the poet Charents as the best Armenian writer of the time, inextricably identified with the nation that bore and nurtured him, which gave him his inspiration, his dreams, his genius, along with his tribulations. Part of that nation denied his existence for eighteen years, only to relent with the painful realization of the injustices forced upon it. He was one with his people, his short life closely paralleling the hard times they experienced. He was both cursed and blessed for having been born in 1897 in the heart of historic Armenia, Kars. Conceived during the massacres of 1896, a witness and chronicler of the 1915 genocide—truly a "Danteesque Legend"—a volunteer in the batallion of Commander Ishkhan Arghoutian, enlisting to help liberate his "blue-eyed fatherland," a devout believer and participant in the 1917 October Revolution, Charents was eventually devoured by another terror, the Stalinist purges. Charents foresaw and, more poignantly than any other writer, wrote about the pestilential *ouragan* (hurricane) that swept the country, and destroyed so many of its children. He wrote with unwavering courage, spurning the expedient rationalizations for compromise many others resorted to. Even these could not save them in the end.

It is possible of course that Gostan Zarian's description of Charents in *The Traveller & His Road*[1] as an obnoxious, gun-toting pest is accurate. But not much is offered to corroborate the characterization, and Zarian himself was self-centered, with prejudices that may have made it difficult for him to acknowledge the genius he had come to observe and write about. Saroyan was a young man when he met Charents; though he may have made references to him later as a "lunatic," he did not fail to grant his genius as well. But then Saroyan was confident enough in his own talent to be able to acknowledge the attributes of another writer.

Charents remained in Armenia after the Soviet regime was established, instead of leaving as many others chose to do; and the politically acrimonious environment that existed abroad affected the perceptions of some contemporary writers.

Charents' early poems glorified the fresh breath the Russian revolution was meant to bring. His "Frenzied Masses," "Lenin," "The Story of Peasant Sako," the "Radio Poems" and others were written in exultant anticipation of wondrous days. Charents believed, or wanted to believe, in the precepts of the revolution; he wanted to be in tune with the fantastic upheavals raging around him. He had proclaimed his credo: "If you wish to have your song heard, then be the breath of your time." He could not have done otherwise. At the age of eighteen, he had witnessed the devastation of his own country and the brutal slaughter of his people; he could not have allowed himself not to anticipate the imprisonment of his fatherland in the "Red Storm" surging down from the northern steppes.

Charents may be regarded as the founder of modern Soviet Armenian literature; he created the standards by which every subsequent writer is measured. There were certainly other fine writers in his time, but none of them achieved his stature. Still others of his contemporaries, like Terenig Temirjian, Vahan Totovents and Stepan Zorian, were already established writers who belonged at least in part to the old pre-revolutionary world. Hovhaness Toumanian was among them, but by 1920 he had already produced his life's work, and would die three years after the Soviet regime emerged. Similarly, Issahakian was a popular poet when he immigrated to Armenia in 1936, and did not produce any major work after that. Perhaps Derian might have excelled Charents as the pre-eminent writer of Soviet Armenia had he not died in 1920. But, by whatever accidents of history, Charents appears to have been destined to lead the new literature of Armenia into untraveled paths.

His two poems, "Danteesque Legend" and "Frenzied Masses," published in 1916 and 1918 respectively, had brought some degree of recognition to their author. In the chaotic days of 1919, the Republic's Minister of Culture and the country's leading literary critic Nigol

Aghbalian, delivered a lecture in Parliament Hall on the new poet, Eghishe Charents. For such an official to give such a lecture in such circumstances was an event in itself. A sense of the bleakness of the life at that time may be derived from an article by Neville Chater published in a 1919 issue of the "National Geographic Magazine":

"To behold misery in Tiflis [capital of the Republic of Georgia] one must search it out. In Erevan one cannot escape it . . . Utter silence brooded over Alexandropol [now Leninakan, second largest city of Armenia], a silence profound and sinister, as if the whole town were muffled out of respect for continuous burial . . . Etchmiadzin contains 7,000 refugees, of whom 1,000 are dying each month."

In spite of the widespread misery, there was determination and optimism in the land. Writers were similarly imbued with this mood; and Charents was at the forefront. He soon sought and gathered around him a nucleus of young poets and novelists, and encouraged them to write; he himself would make sure their work was published. And when a book was printed, he would call the author and personally hand him the first copy off the press. In addition he supervised the publication of children's books, paying particular attention to their appearance. He brought together a group of distinguished literary critics and historians under the direction of Manoog Abeghian, to prepare the definitive edition of the Armenian national epic, *David of Sassoun*.

Between 1920 and 1930 Charents published several books of poetry and two novels, constantly experimenting to develop a style best suited to the expression of the historic changes around him. The new life needed a new literary language, a new medium to be in harmony with the mood of the times. He even tried the theater and film in order to capture the new fervor that possessed the country, which seemed to compensate for the material deprivation being experienced.

The bleakness of life served as a counterpoint to the determination of artists and scholars like Charents, Makintsian, and Bakounts to make the best of it with the little they had, to create the best from virtually nothing which only intensified their disillusionment a decade later when they came to realize that they had been deceived, exploited by a leader who had corrupted the system for which they had fought. Whether this development was aberrant or intrinsically part of the system was not of immediate concern to them. The obscenity of the crimes perpetrated against them made the distinction irrelevant; no amount of clarification or self-justification would bring back those who perished in the Siberian gulags.

Large numbers of Armenian intellectuals—writers, artists, scientists—were sacrificed at the whim of a despot. Some of them survived. The best, Bakounts and Charents, did not. We shall never be able to reconcile ourselves to this immense loss, just as we shall never know where the remains of Charents and Bakounts lie buried. The country they loved, for the liberation of which they fought while still in their teens, could not mark their graves with a slab of marble.

As director of the State Press, it appears, from all available memoirs, that Charents was scrupulously fair. His judgment of a new manuscript was based solely on its inherent quality; it did not matter whether the author was friend or foe. And he did have opponents, though he was himself a formidable antagonist; he could silence anyone with his wit and biting sarcasm. He did not resort to devious intrigues; he fought openly and bravely, and was finally defeated by the treachery of his detractors whose principal strength derived from their servility before the authorities. We will return to this later. In determining whether or not to publish a book, he relied on his own instincts, Bakounts being the only writer whose opinion he sometimes sought. Once a decision was made, the books would be processed quickly. Writers like Mekertich Armen, Karekin Bess, and Khachig Tashdents had their first work published through the encouragement and initiative of Charents. His responsibilities at the press drained most of Charents' energies and time, leaving very little of either for his own writing. Still, when Charents' complete works were published in the 1960s, they amounted to six volumes of 400 to 500 pages each. A final volume of some 700 pages was issued in 1983, containing the work he had done after 1933, the greater part of which had not been published during his lifetime. In a relatively short span of forty years, he left an impressive literary legacy, suggesting that he worked almost incessantly, without being discouraged by other obligations, or by the constant and often cruel criticism he was subjected to during the last three or four years of his life.

In writing about Charents some tend to stress the point that he was a communist. Mrs. Helen Puzand, a contemporary of Charents, doubts that Charents joined the party in 1918, as some of his biographers would have us believe. But the date is hardly the point; he was a communist and it does not much matter when he joined. What matters is that he joined because he believed the regime would protect an Armenia whose very existence was at stake, and not necessarily because he possessed a true believer's fervor. Charents sought a safe haven for the survivors of the holocaust. And that is what he saw in the new order. Had not Charents' mentor Aghbalian predicted that "Armenia will eventually Armenianize communism just as she did with Christianity?" It is true that his early work glorified the revolution; but no other Armenian writer proved more earnestly nationalistic, or a greater Armenian patriot. To some the word "nationalist" is a pejorative term; Charents elevated the term to its purest and most noble implications. One can more accurately describe Charents as a humanist, but that may be too broad to be meaningful.

The Book of the Road, Charents' last work, is a poet's patriotic canvas of luminous vistas glittering with metaphors; the reader is drawn into their vertiginous whirl as the poet's vibrant voice sometimes laments, sometimes glorifies a past both heroic and tragic. Along with this volume, Charents' last poems written betweeen 1934 to his death on November 29, 1937 (incidentally, the 17th anniversary of the Soviet regime in Armenia), and first published in Erevan in 1983, represent a complete departure from his early revolutionary work. In these poems Charents develops further the thematic shift begun in The Book of the Road; while the style may sometimes appear diffuse, the briskness and lucidity of the poet's voice are unmistakably, uniquely Charentsian. The symbolism is far less oblique, to the point of seeming obvious. The poet had made his choice, crossing the ideological and political Rubicon in a critical transition, and could not concern himself with the consequences. The totality of the indomitable Armenian poet rises like a huge "Eiffelian Tower," as he had expressed it in another context, to stand guard over whatever Charents had inherited of Armenian culture. If there was any doubt about his patriotism, it was put to rest by his long poem, "In Memory of N.S.," cited here in translation. It first appeared in Kragan Tert in Erevan in 1967, and understandably is not included in the 1983 volume of his previously unpublished work. In it Charents audaciously reaffirms the indestructibility of the Armenian spirit:

Mysterious, insoluble, taut
element not subject to union
with foreign elements which
have flooded it for centuries,
self generating light from the dawn
of time, from the source of light until now

you, Nayirian embryo, perhaps now
you have finally reached the hour of labor
pains?

* * *

I sing praises to the wild powers
of destruction which became teachers
of disaster, of desertion, and disappearance,
without leaving their mark.
Finally I will sing praises
to the fearful Nayirian spirit
which greeted death by refuting
that which came to destroy.

* * *

Death can be joyful,
a march, superbly victorious,
a festive cortege toward the future
through the stunning cold,
trailing glory, glory of the embryo,
thousands of embryos flying in the face of death.

But you who are confused, dishevelled and
dying, dying before your deaths,
in living death, you who eat the bread
of cringing, self-abnegating,
bowing before the maniacal scythe,
that cuts you down—stand up.

He had heralded the "red dawn"; he had fought for it. When it betrayed his expectations, when he realized the emptiness of the promise, and witnessed its subjection to the vagaries of an individual's neurosis, he did not hesitate to break with it:

And it is the old sun again returning
from the West, like Lazarus risen
from death's coffin—the sun would return . . .[2]

These lines addressed in his solitude to the eleventh-century poet Krikor Naregatsi, might lead one to think of Charents in despair. It would be a mistake, for Charents never lost his optimism about the eventual triumph of the Armenian spirit, in spite of his awareness of impending danger. He was fired as director of the State Press, and people began avoiding him as if he had an infectious disease.

The friend and mentor of almost every writer of any consequence, Charents was left without friends, except for a few loyal intimates who visited him occasionally.

Was Charents' seemingly resurgent nationalism and response to the powerful bonds that linked him to his nation's culture and traditions due to the persecutions he had endured? Or was it simply that he still held the instinctive belief that he could find consolation and serenity only in his beginnings—on those benches in the parks in Kars, for example, where during his adolescent years he had read Khorenatsi's *History of the Armenians*, the epic story of a past long gone? Curiously there is a reference to the historian in an entry Charents made in his diary on his 40th birthday, while he was in prison. It is clear that Charents' patriotic feelings were not at any time diminished. His attachment to the fifth century poets, historians, and scholars, themselves supreme nationalists by virtue of their creation of the Armenian alphabet and the nationalization of Christianity, is one indication of this. His references to Khorenatsi reaffirmed his regard for him as a symbol with which he could identify. A comparable mood prevails in his novel, *Erkir Nayiri*, written in 1922, long before his persecution had gathered fatal momentum. Though sometimes satirical, it is an agonizing recreation of the first fall of the fortress city of Kars, Charents' birthplace, on April 17, 1918. He has detailed the customs, the habits, and the work of the city, along with the intrigues and jealousies of the municipal leadership; the life of a bustling Armenian city forever gone, along with the shameful failure of will in the defense of the city, the fatherland. Charents knew the city well and could not have conceived of the cowardice of the military defenders that eventually had tragic consequences. Mazooti Hamo, the central character of the book, sometimes seems like a picaresque figure; yet towards the end, as the soldiers flee, Hamo achieves the heroic in his futile effort to stop the retreat, to save the city, the "last king-like Nayirtsi," as Charents describes him, desperately trying to evoke a heroic past for a people who, in a frenzy of fear, can think of nothing beyond saving their own skins. The city falls, and Hamo and a few other leaders are taken prisoners and crucified. The second fall of Kars on October 31, 1920, is one of the eerie mysteries of our recent past. The same people only two years earlier had turned back the onslaught of a Turkish army intent on wiping out the last remnant of whatever was left of Armenia; an entire nation led by the Catholicos and the folk hero Aram Manoukian had fought valiantly for the historic land that would later become present-day Armenia. But by 1920 Aram had died of typhoid, and there was no central figure who could galvanize the country. It is questionable whether even Aram could have made a difference in face of the political intrigues which auctioned off Armenia's interests for the glory of the proletarian revolution, as detailed by the historian Borian in a book published in the least likely of places, Moscow. Charents could not have remained indifferent to those momentous days which provided so vivid a backdrop to his writing. His hopes of ever seeing a liberated Kars were dashed by successive treaties in 1921 between the Soviet Union and Turkey, treaties that formalized the usurpation of Armenian provinces, actually all of Western Armenia, and sealed the boundaries. He may indeed have been a devout communist, having seen in the rise of the "red dawn" the liberation of his homeland; but when that did not materialize, when he could no longer escape the feeling of having been deceived, his disillusionment and grief found immediate expression in the work he produced from 1933 until his death in 1937. It is in this context that the patriotism and alienation of Charents must be considered. To ascribe Charents' morphine addiction solely to the harassment he was subjected to, misses the point. In fact he became addicted following a kidney operation while he was still a celebrated poet and public figure. His alienation from the system derived mainly from the fact that his expectations for his country simply did not materialize. Whether he would have succumbed to morphine addiction even without the operation no one can know.

What we do know is that he remained faithful to his innermost instincts, gave expression to the grief that his nation tried so hard to contain, ignored the impending danger to his own life, and did not deviate from his patriotism for expedient considerations. In the process he became the conscience of his nation, during his lifetime and after.

Charents wrote his last poem on a napkin on the night of September 27, 1937, two months before his death in prison. It is a relatively short poem dedicated to Avetik Issahakian. He was moved to write the poem, he explains, while listening to a prisoner singing one of Issahakian's songs. In an accompanying note he assures Issahakian that he is alert and in good spirits, and that his family's fate remains his chief concern, about which he could do nothing but trust them to God and the Armenian nation. The poem, however, goes beyond a simple obeisance to the elder poet whom he admired. It may have been triggered by Issahakian's song, but it is the last searingly moving tribute Charents paid to the culture he loved and enriched. He wanted to write a poem as simple as Issahakian's on his cell wall where it would remain forever for successive generations to read and be able to share the warm music of his heart. Two months and two days later, Charents' life ended in a prison in Erevan. We know nothing about the circumstances. The writer Vagharshag Norents, himself a prisoner in a nearby cell, was to write: "I have never before nor ever since heard such a cry. It was the last time I heard Charents' voice." It is rumored that Charents, in a fit of despair, crushed his own head against the prison wall. If it is so, he may have spared a wretched prison guard the dubious distinction of being the executioner who silenced his country's voice of conscience.

Charents need not have envied Issahakian. He did not have to inscribe anything on the walls of his prison cell. Whatever he wrote, from his "Blue-Eyed Fatherland" to his last poems, is indelibly imprinted on the hearts of every generation of Armenians that came after him, and will be in those that are still to come. We may never know where he was buried, or whether he has a grave at all, but every young Armenian schoolchild who recites his verses is a living monument to his work. As long as there is an Armenian who can read him in his own language, the endless wealth of which Charents so lovingly mined, the luminous beauty of which he revealed to us, Charents will need no other monument.

[1] In the English translation of Zarian's work, this essay was included in the volume, *Bancoop & the Bones of the Mammoth*, Ashod Press, New York, 1981.
[2] Translations are from *Land of Fire* by Diana Der Hovanessian and Marzbed Margossian, Ardis Press, Ann Arbor, Michigan, 1985. For a detailed biography of Charents, see "Eghishe Charents: His Life, His Poetry, and His Times" by Diana Der Hovanessian and Marzbed Margossian, in the Winter 1979 issue of "Ararat."

ACROSS TWO WORLDS

Erevan's House of Correction

The book from which these segments have been translated was written in March and April of 1927, and first published in Tiflis in the same year under the title, *Memoirs of Erevan's House of Correction.* On September 5, 1926, on Abovian Street, Charents flirted with a woman by the name of Aivazian. When she spurned his advances, Charents shot and wounded her. He was arrested, tried, and on November 9 sentenced to eight years in prison, with strict solitary confinement. But because the woman survived, and because the effect of such a harsh sentence on Charents would have been profound, the sentence was reduced to three years, without solitary confinement. The death of his wife on December 29, 1926, had a considerable psychological impact on him. A panel of psychiatrists examined Charents on January 8, 1927, and recommended his removal to a sanatorium. He left the prison in February of that year and went to Maikob, near his mother and brothers, to convalesce.

The writer Zabelle Yessayan was present at the trial, and wrote about it in the Paris paper, "Erevan," late in 1926. She described Charents as depressed and distracted, "his eyes fixed on a stack of papers," noting his own testimony about his desperate condition, his unrelieved insomnia, and the constant nightmares from which he sought relief in alcohol. It was this condition that had apparently led him to commit "so sorrowful and regrettable an act." She found Charents convincing, "his voice sometimes emotional . . . and with no doubt that the accused is sincere." He had made no effort to justify himself.

Charents effectively evokes the life and conditions of the prison. There are all kinds of characters, drawn from widely differing social strata—political prisoners, felons, petty thieves. From his descriptions, however, the House of Correction seems more like a rehabilitation center than a prison. In any event, there is no sense of the harsh circumstances that most certainly prevailed in later years.

At the time of his imprisonment, Charents was already regarded as the leading writer of his time, his revolutionary and other poems were well known, his novel *Erkir Nayiri,* had been published the year before and had been critically acclaimed. He was in the circumstances, hardly an ordinary prisoner; this might explain the apparently privileged status he enjoyed, and the freedom of movement allowed him.

The memoir was first serialized in the Tiflis daily, "Mardagoch," and published there in book form soon after.

The inmates remembered the House of Correction's warden, Hemayag Chakhmakhjian (1891-1963), with affection and admiration, speaking warmly of his character, of his gentle and considerate attitude towards the prisoners, and especially towards Charents.

If his first imprisonment was rather uneventful, even if sometimes depressing, the second time was an experience of an entirely different character. Times had changed dramatically, and for the worst.

Erevan's House of Correction

On September 5, 1926, at midnight, I was arrested for a very serious offense, and taken to the criminal sector of the Erevan police station. After being detained there for an entire week, one dusty, windy evening I was transferred, in the company of the Erevan police chief, to the House of Correction, which was situated across from the so-called "New Station," next to the armory.

Until that day I had no idea whatever about our houses of correction; I had never been in any of them. I knew only that some old prisons had been converted into such places; but what they actually represented was as vague and uncertain to me as the night of my arrest was dark and forbidding, the night the police van stopped in front of those closed gates long enough for me to read, in the dim headlights of the van, the square plaque mounted to the left of the gate:

N. K. Zh. G.
House of Correction of the Republic

There was an iron knocker on the door of the gate. When the police chief rapped on it, a small window to the left of the door opened immediately, revealing the face of a man in a military cap. A few words were exchanged in a low voice, the door was opened, and we entered the House of Correction, first me, then the police chief. In other circumstances, being the first to enter could be interpreted as a sign of respect; but here, of course, the implication was understandably different! The environment was oppressive; a misty, hallucinatory image of Feodor Dostoevsky's *The House of the Dead* shot through my mind, and it suddenly seemed that life, the world, all my ties, all my acquaintances, even the sun and the blue sky, were left behind us, on the other side of that locked gate, and whatever it was that awaited me on this side was still unknown to me, and the not knowing was painfully depressing.

"To the left!" the police chief directed, and we turned left to enter the hospital of the House of Correction, where I was assigned to one of the so-called "isolation rooms." The police chief nodded and left. The door closed and I was left alone. It was a small room, furnished only with an iron bed and a chair. Small rooms have always depressed me. I don't know why, but I have always delighted in large rooms, huge halls in fact, without any furniture to speak of. A bed, a chair, a desk, these are all the furnishings I have ever dreamt of or required. From this viewpoint, then, I didn't have much to complain about. Only the desk was missing, and I could ask for that the next day. The room had another kind of advantage which compensated partly for the deficiency of its size; it had an extremely high ceiling, something I find very satisfying. When the police chief was gone, the first thing I did was measure the size of the room: eight feet by four. Then I studied the lamp, hanging very high, so high that no one could possibly reach it, even if he were to stand on a chair. "It had to be lowered a little, if I was to do any work at all,"

I mused, but later I learned that it was deliberately kept out
of reach. Who knows what kind of prisoners were confined
in this "isolation room" who would be able to harm
themselves in a moment of depression? I almost forgot to men-
tion the window. It was large and overlooked the courtyard.
I wasn't sure whether we were permitted to open it at night,
and since in such places one is more likely to assume most
things are forbidden, I simply assumed that this also might
be; so I thought I would wait until the next day to find out
what there was outside. By then I would be better acquainted
with the rules and regulations.

"So this is the House of Correction," I thought, after study-
ing the room for a time. Seated on the bed, I stared at the
opposite wall. It was quiet. There were no sounds at all. It
must have been seven o'clock in the evening; I began wonder-
ing how I would get through the night. "And suppose I some-
how manage to make it till morning," I thought, "what
about the next day and the one after that? And who knows
how many more such nights there are to be?" The most
dreaded enemy man has in this world, boredom, began to close
around my chest. It is possible to get used to sadness, to ac-
commodate to it somehow; it is possible to live with
hopelessness and grief; but to suffer boredom is to succumb
to death. "I wonder what is happening in the other cells,"
I thought, my mind already probing for ways out of this tiny
world. I got up and went to the window and opened it. What
I saw and heard flooded my being with the kind of elation
a bedouin must feel when he glimpses a green oasis in the
vast parched desert. Across the courtyard I saw a row of
lighted windows; loud voices and laughter came from them,
and music, the sound of songs, mandolins, flutes, kemanchas,
the deep bass of the kemancha the most touching of all, caress-
ing my heart like the sweet melancholy music of a violin. The
sound of the kemancha issued from the first-floor window,
while the other sounds came from the second floor. It seemed
strange to me that some of the upper windows were more

brightly lit than the others. I wondered why. One other thing puzzled me; the music was coming, not from anywhere near the windows, but from deep inside the rooms. Apparently it was not in the outer rooms that the men were singing and playing, but in rooms farther inside. Below, however, the kemancha was obviously being played in the cell that faced the yard. I was still preoccupied with these thoughts when the music suddenly stopped, and the sound of applause tumbled across the courtyard. It could not have come from a single cell; it was too loud for that. It sounded like the clapping of fifteen or twenty men, and even more. It was a puzzle I couldn't figure out. I was imagining all sorts of things, that perhaps the men had been brought together for recreation in a large room or hall, when the applause suddenly stopped, and not a sound emanated from the second floor. The invisible kemancha's sweet cry of oriental sadness, trembling like the voice of a barely adolescent girl, still flowed from the window on the first floor. And I felt that the insufferable boredom that only a moment ago had threatened to suffocate me didn't really exist, that it had already been transformed into a soft sadness in my heart, the kind of sadness that fills human hearts on spring mornings, when men go into the open fields, and look down roads that rush towards distant horizons. The sadness is not oppressive, but light, because it enables men to experience the depth, the immensity of life, to sense that life is limitless, that they bear within themselves inexhaustible possibilities. And it is not paradoxical to say that such sadness is in its essence optimistic; the sort of optimistic sadness with which Beethoven's heroic music is imbued, music Lenin liked so much.[1] Leaning on the window sill of my "isolation room," like a helpless alcoholic I drew in the sadness of the kemancha rushing toward me from across the yard when, from the windows above, the loud applause broke out again and, almost at the same moment, the door of my room opened and a hospital orderly entered.

"Do you want some tea?" he asked, smiling as he added:

"The windows must not be opened at night; it is forbidden."

"What is all that applause?" I asked him, without any hesitation, without closing the window, as I pointed to the windows opposite. "And why is the light brighter there?"

"That is the cultural sector of the House of Correction," he answered. "There is a performance today."

Everything became immediately clear, the songs, the music, the applause, and the silence afterwards.

"Who is playing the kemancha?"

"One of our prisoners, Meno. He plays very well, doesn't he?"

"Very well, comrade, better than well. And how long are they allowed to play?"

"As long as they want; till dawn, if they wish to."

"I don't want tea," I told him. "I would rather you allowed me to keep the window open."

And we arrived at a secret agreement; I could leave the window half-open, if I was careful not to stand near it. Then he went out and closed the door.

"It is not as awful as I thought, or as it was in Uncle Dostoevsky's *House of the Dead,*" I said to myself and, stretching out on the bed, I began to listen to Meno's music. That evening, my first in the House of Correction, I listened to that music for a long time; and the music convinced me that life had not yet ended, that it is in fact inexhaustible, that it carries within itself an endless variety of fragrances and possibilities. Thanks to Meno. And to that hospital orderly who revealed for me the secrets of the music and applause that came from the second floor across the yard. "Here also, people manage to live, as they do outside and, as it appears, have sufficient resources to live and enjoy," I told myself as I stretched out to sleep.

The next morning I awoke in a calmer frame of mind, and from that very day an extraordinary world began to unfold before me, a world that was strange, different, and surprising.

The Criminal Sector

When I entered the office together with the chief of the House of Correction, we found that Nikolaev, the technician whose plans we had come to inspect, had gone somewhere, and was not expected back for an hour. So I left the office and went to take a look at the criminal sector. There was no one I knew yet in the House of Correction, so I went alone.

The entrance to the criminal sector was five paces to the left when I came out of the office. The huge wooden door had a flimsy lock that looked ridiculously inappropriate.

The door was shut, but a prisoner stood before it with a key in his hand. I was astonished. How could they entrust the key to a prisoner? "But perhaps it was not just any prisoner," I thought, the poor soul evoking harsh images of a pitiless Cerberus in my mind. I learned later that my doubts were unfounded. The gate of the criminal sector had no connection to the internal security system of the House of Correction. The only reason it was kept shut was to prevent prisoners from going to the hospital and the office without permission, where they might add to the confusion, and disturb the work. The most inept prisoners were usually assigned to that post because their function was no more than that of a doorman.

"Can I go in?"

He pushed the door open immediately—the lock was open, and merely hooked through the rings—and I entered the yard of the criminal sector.

Directly opposite was a one-story building. After taking a few steps towards it, I turned to my right, where the baths and the kitchen of the House of Correction were located.

At the kitchen and the bath too, which was not in use that day, I came across various prisoners, as I had earlier, some alone, some in small groups. Their eyes seemed to be searching mine, making me a little uncomfortable. I found myself staring at them, too. They seemed to me inaccessible beings, withdrawn into themselves, harsh and unlikable, with whom it did not seem possible to be friends, or create any sort of human relationship. They recalled the protagonists of Dostoevsky and Toroshevich, and my sense of loneliness intensified. I wondered if I would ever be able to pass among these men, and be greeted naturally with a smile? At the moment that was my one dream, as I instinctively made my way along the wall, determined not to disturb or distract them. How could I know that many of them, almost all of them in fact, were quite ordinary, sociable men, and that in a week many of them would be my comrades and friends. Of course the friendships would have a casual character, like those made on a train, when one goes on a long journey, or at the front.

The bath was closed, and there was nothing special about the kitchen: Huge copper kettles, like the ones we had in the armory; a few prisoners wearing kitchen garb, one of them pouring water in the kettles, a few others peeling potatoes. That was all, and with nothing to keep me there, I soon headed for the criminal sector.

Ahead was the vast courtyard, almost the size of a small field. It was separated from the walls of the House of Correction with a fence of barbed wire strung on wooden posts, set some four paces from the wall. Armed soldiers were on guard along the fence.

Beyond the walls, in the distance, were the grey hills of Erevan, turning a copper-red in the evening. They reminded me of the vast free world outside, and I suddenly felt myself an orphan, alone, cut off from everything.

I looked around me. Some prisoners sat in groups near the fence, others walked about as they chatted. None of them knew me as yet, keeping their distance stubbornly, it seemed to me; still, much like a naked man strolling along a boulevard, I was the object of curious and contemptuous attention. This is the feeling their long scrutinizing stares aroused in me; it was difficult for me to discern in those stares merely curiosity about a newcomer, especially a newcomer they might have heard some rumors about.

I continued until I reached the criminal sector. I looked at the men as I went by, trying to guess the kind of crime that brought each of them to this place. But those who at first glance evoked images of merciless bandits and vicious murderers turned out, when I came to know them, to be the least reprehensible of the prisoners. The contrary was also true. Almost all those who had made no impression on me at all, who had appeared utterly harmless, as if condemned to this place by some tragic misunderstanding, wretched and pitiable men—they were the ones convicted of the most serious crimes.

From the outset, I was affected by the harshness of the criminal sector. The iron door to the entrance, the tiled flooring of the corridors, the thick walls, and the oppressive roundness of the cells, these were enough to dishearten any newcomer. It had been the czarist provincial jail, with its dismal formal czarist style. Who knows what things have been done here, in these corridors, when the czarist guards and wardens were in charge? How many souls suffered and perished? I wondered as I looked around me. Though the corridors were adequately lighted, they still seemed dull with a somber darkness, an airless oppression. My reaction might have been different if I had entered the sector not alone for the first time, but in the company of some friend.

On the lower floor of the criminal sector, I came to a closed door, near which a guard sat on a wooden chair.

"What is behind that door?" I asked the guard.

"Secrets," he answered cryptically, "the secrets of the lower floor," and considered that sufficient explanation. I learned later that there, and on the floor above, were the isolation cells where those arrested were detained for questioning until their trials, after which they were either transferred to the regular prison cells or released.

I turned back and went toward the other end of the corridor. There were only five cells in this area; their doors were open and the prisoners went in and out freely. There were no guards except the one who sat in front of the isolation cells.

I entered the first cell which was at the end of the corridor. A staircase there led upstairs to the cultural division.

It was a bright and spacious room with huge windows, the walls lined with about twenty wooden benches. The walls and the ceiling were white and clean. An electric lamp hung from a wire in the center of the ceiling. The floor looked as though it had just been mopped. The room was empty, but for two prisoners who were seated in a corner chatting. When I entered, they got up to greet me.

"Who uses this room?"

"Prisoners." They smiled, as if to say the answer was obvious and hardly required explanation.

"Then where are they?"

"At work. We are the only ones without jobs in this section. I clean up the place; as for him, he's not well, and can't work."

"Where do they work?"

"In the masonry shop, and some in the craft shops outside."

"Why were you convicted?"

"For robbery," he answered, smiling again. He was in his early twenties, and had the look of a peasant. His face had a yellowish cast, and his eyes kept blinking.

"And you?" I asked the other.

"I'm from Shenogh," he said curtly, as if that was enough to explain everything. And apparently it was. Later I found that all the inmates who were from the village of Shenogh had been imprisoned for the same deed, the widely-publicized deviation of its local leadership.

I soon made my way into the other rooms, all the same size, all with about twenty cots. In none of them were there more than two or three people. The rest were either in the yard or at work.

I went upstairs. It was the same there, except for a few

Turkish prisoners, all peasants, who attracted my attention. One other thing became quickly apparent. The bedding and other belongings of the prisoners were inferior to what I had seen below. Some cots had no mattresses at all, only torn rags or burlap sacks. On the lower floors, almost three-fourths of the cots were covered with home-made mattresses, with colorful home-made bed covers and white pillows. Obviously the inmates on the upper floor were poorer than the others. As for cleanliness, it was the same in all areas. Nowhere could you find even a discarded match, or a cigarette butt crushed out on the floor.

While I was busy absorbing these preliminary impressions, prisoners kept moving in and out, all the time scrutinizing me suspiciously from head to toe. I kept thinking about the prisoners I had come across as I started out, attempting to arrange them into groups according to their outer appearances. Most of those I saw inside were also peasants, and almost half of them Turks. Then, there were the thieves and beggars from the towns, like the ones I used to see so often in the western part of Erevan near the Zankou River, in the cafes, beer houses, and shops. If Erevan has its "unsavory corners," it is from there that these men came. I used to wander about those districts often, in the early mornings, or evenings after dark, intrigued by the dark, strange, filthy areas which reminded me of the dens depicted in detective fiction. The people of those dismal places bear a recognizable character for anyone who has even the slightest familiarity with them. And here, in the criminal sector of Erevan's House of Correction, I met a considerable number of such men. And I was not mistaken. Many of those on the upper floor were offenders who had been returned to prison repeatedly and, as I was able to confirm later, protagonists of those "dark corners." I got to know most them, found them rather primitive and, in their way, interesting people—Balthasar, Lazki, Macho, Khouzhan-Khacho, Hussein, Valo . . .

Then came the former Soviet civil servants, whom the

other prisoners labelled "intellectual." The one or two soldiers I met that day could be counted among that group.

These preliminary judgments of the inmates of the House of Correction proved to be generally accurate, as I found when I got better acquainted with them.

Peasants, bums, and former civil servants, these comprised the principal social strata of the criminal sector. Of course, as later observations clarified, it could not have been any other way; further, each of these groups could have been subdivided in turn, especially the peasants. There were the destitute peasants, and there were kulaks, who had no role in the internal order of the imates. The peasants lived according to their customs, the bums according to theirs, and civil servants to theirs. Their behavior as prisoners also interested me. They were isolated, cut off from the outer world; and here, besides the customary social rules, there had to be other special laws which related to the particular conditions of the House of Correction. There had to be considerations that pertained only to prisoners, with no relation to experiences outside, based only on an understanding of the prisoners' existence and moral standards inside. For me, before anything, it was necessary to develop an understanding of these standards and existence, in order to broach the center of that society, become an equal in it, penetrate its depth and its psychology . . .

With such thoughts going through my mind, I went back into the yard where some prisoners still loitered. Yes, peasants, bums, and former civil servants. They walked about, stopped here and there, chatted, while I stood alone and speculated on which of these three groups controlled the internal regime of the prison, not the administration of course, but the conduct, the relationships, the life itself. Which element of this colorful society represented the internal power that set the standards and enforced them within the framework supervised by the officials of the House of Correction? There had to be men with influence, the leaders, and I was attempting to guess which of those surrounding me could be among them.

But a sense of loneliness was closing in on me, and I thought it best to return to the office. Besides it was time to go to the chief's office to examine the plans for the new craft shops. And I hurried, as though suddenly reminded of some urgent business that had to be attended to immediately.

Darcho and Balthasar: Variations on a Theme

It was a Sunday, and my wife Arpenig had come to visit me.

I had not shaved for three days, so I needed one badly. I knew about the barbershop in the building where the bath was, so I asked the hospital orderly to summon the barber. A few minutes later the door of my room opened, and the barber walked in, his head uncovered, wearing a white apron, and carrying a razor and other tools of his trade.

He was about thirty years old, slightly taller than average, and pale; he had blue eyes, and blond wavy hair, neatly combed. From his bland appearance it was hard to tell what kind of a man he was. His dialect marked him as a native of Tiflis.

When he finished shaving me and began to cut my hair, it seemed the right time to start on my usual questioning.

"Why were you arrested?"

"For murder."

"How did it happen?"

"It just happened. There was some bitter feeling, and it ended with my killing him."

"Where?"

"Right here in Erevan. Actually a man and a woman. The man was old, the woman younger. He didn't go easily, I'll tell you that."

"How did you do it? Were you alone?"

"Alone. I went into the house at night, and locked the door behind me. Only the man and his wife were there. He was in one room, the wife in another. I killed the man first, and then the woman."

"How?"

"The man with a knife, the woman with my hands. I held her by the throat, and in no time she was gone, without the slightest trouble or noise."

"Why didn't you kill her with a knife too?"

"What's the matter with you? Is she a man to be killed with a knife? For a woman the hands are used to strangle her, here like this."

He made a half-circle with the thumb and index finger of his right hand and demonstrated how a woman should be strangled. My wife seemed hypnotized by his contorted face. The poor woman was horrified.

"That's how it was done. I stayed there more than two hours. I had locked the door and put the keys in my pocket. I didn't want the neighbors to think there was anything wrong; it was best if they thought no one was at home, that the old man and woman had gone out."

"What were you doing there so long?"

"I was waiting for it to get dark. As soon as it was dark, I left."

"Then how were you caught?"

"In the city. I didn't have identification papers. They were suspicious and arrested me. Then everything came unravelled."

"What was the verdict?"

"I was going to be executed. Then the Central Committee changed the sentence to ten years, as soon as they found out they could profit from the crime."

"Profit?"

"Yes, when they searched the house, they discovered more than 150 pieces of gold. That made them go easier on me."

I smiled, but he pretended not to notice my reaction.
"What's your name?"

"Darcho. I am from Shulaver. I didn't want to come to
Erevan. It was to settle that old account that I came, only for
that."

My wife could restrain herself no longer.

"Didn't your conscience disturb you for killing those poor
people? Doesn't it bother you now?"

Darcho's surprise quickly turned to contempt.

"Conscience? What need is there for a conscience?
Especially where such miserable people are involved? What
is a man, anyway, dear sister? No more than the squealing
offspring of a chicken. Grab him once by the throat and he's
finished."

And with almost angelic serenity, Darcho resumed his
clipping. When he finished, he gathered his utensils, bundling
them in the apron, and left. As soon as he was out of the
room, my wife hugged me, as though protecting me from im-
minent danger:

"Dearest Charents, don't ever let him shave you again;
he'll slice off your head."

Poor Arpenig. She didn't know the real story about Dar-
cho's crime, and I never had the opportunity to tell her about
it later. She didn't know how deviously the tongue is used
in the world of the prisoners, true disciples of the wisdom
of diplomats, believing that the tongue was intended to disguise
rather than express their real thoughts and deeds.

Darcho's story had its effect on me too. Don't forget that
I was just entering that world, just beginning to know the peo-
ple who still regarded me, not as one of them, but as an "in-
tellectual," someone to be mocked and impressed in turn with
tales of terrifying deeds they had not actually committed.

When I saw Benjamin that evening, I told him about my
talk with Darcho. He looked me up and down, sneering at
my credulity, and answered curtly:

"Don't believe him. Don't believe a word he said."

"Why? What reason does he have to lie to me?"

"He was lying, all right. First of all, he wasn't alone on that job."

"Who else was in on it?"

"There were four of them, him and his friends Balthasar, Oss, and Hamo."

"Which Balthasar?"

"The one in charge of the House of Correction. And Hamo is the blacksmith. He's an actor and stage designer too. As for Oss, he makes tools in the blacksmith's shop. Go find out from them."

We ran into Balthasar a little later in the corridor of the cultural activities section. I remembered having seen him in the school, in the Turkish class, where he attracted my attention with his virile appearance.

A well-built youth, he was tall, broad-shouldered, his face bronzed as if a light mist hung over it. In spite of this appearance of strength and self-confidence, he blinked with embarrassment when I stared at him. He spoke sufficiently good Armenian and Russian, but he was obviously not educated. He was certainly not an intellectual, but neither was he an ordinary laborer. He was the typical loafer, raised in the city, clever and opportunistic. Among the prisoners, he enjoyed a reputation for bravery and daring. I learned later that he was proud of that reputation, and would do anything to protect it. More, being recognized as a brave man had become the one ideal, even obsession, of his life.

Benjamin introduced us. I told him Darcho's story and, like Benjamin, he responded curtly, though he smiled as he spoke.

"He is lying."

"Please tell me about it if you can. I would like very much to know about it."

"Why not?"

And there, standing in the corridor, simply and coherently, earnestly and calmly, he related the tragic story, which seemed far removed from him now and drained of all emotional content.

"I was working in the stockroom of the synthetic textiles plant; I used to open the cartons," Balthasar began his story. "But they fired me. I was out of work for a while. It was then that I met Darcho and we got to be friends. He was jobless too. He had come from Tiflis and was looking for work. We were in a tavern one day, and he told me about a job we could do, if I was man enough. He introduced me to Hamo and Oss who were working in a blacksmith's shop, Hamo as a foreman, and Oss as an apprentice. They told us that the shopowner had a lot of money in his house, and other things of value too. It was just him and his wife, and he was a stingy, old man always sucking at the soul of his workers. He cut their pay when he felt like it, and sometimes didn't even pay them at all. We agreed to do the job, waiting only for an opportune moment. Our plan was to go to his house one night, on the pretext that Hamo and Oss wanted to get their pay because they wanted to go to Tiflis; as their friends we were simply tagging along. And that's what we did. It was Sunday evening, about six o'clock. We went to their house. A policeman was patrolling the street nearby. We closed the door behind us. Hamo said they had come to get the money so they could go to Tiflis. It was him and the old wife in the room. There was no one else. He looked suspicious, but said nothing. I winked at Oss, then grabbed the old man, and as soon as I did, Oss struck with the knife. He did not die immediately, so I stuffed a towel into his mouth to keep him from screaming. Darcho and Hamo strangled the woman at the same time. The wife went very quickly. As soon as they covered her face, she was gone. We began to search the rooms. We found nothing. I told them not to take things like clothing, things that could be identified easily, but they didn't listen. Darcho took the man's coat. There was some silver which I gathered into a small bundle. Darcho went to see if the policeman was still there. He did not return. Then Hamo and Oss went. Finally

I left with the package in my hand. I had barely taken a few
steps before the policeman spotted me. He shouted at me to
stop. I didn't. I turned into a side street, the policeman right
behind me. There was no way out. I threw the package away,
jumped over a fence into the adjoining yard, and from there
into another yard. I took off my coat and threw it over my
shoulder, stuffed my hat into my pocket, and went out into
the street, only to run into the same policeman. He asked me
if I had seen such and such a man. I said no, I hadn't. He
didn't look around anymore, and went away. I turned into
the next street. I was free.''

"Then how were you caught?''

"Because of Oss' stupidity. He got on the train to Tiflis
without a pass. But even that he might have gotten away with.
Then he got off at the same station, and walked straight into
the interrogation room. He doesn't know why himself, the
idiot. Well, they grabbed him immediately and questioned
him. They had already heard about the murder. He didn't have
any papers, so they arrested him and sent him to the criminal
sector here. It wasn't long before Oss confessed, but he didn't
betray us. Still they managed to trace us through him. We
were supposed to be shot, but they changed the sentence to
ten years.''

"Why?'' I wanted to know Balthasar's view of this, since
Darcho's was hardly a reasonable one.

"Because we confessed, I suppose. Choubar convinced
us to confess. He said if you confess, they'll commute the
sentence. So we confessed.''

He was silent for a while, then added:

"They also took our circumstances into consideration, and
the shopowner's. He was an evil man, and everybody knew
it.''

Balthasar told all this in a calm tone, with an indifference
that seemed to remove him from the event, all the while look-
ing straight into my eyes, while rapidly blinking his.

"But why are you so curious?'' he suddenly asked when

he finished the story. I sensed a suspicion in Balthasar's eyes that I couldn't quite understand.

"It is just that, Balthasar. Curiosity."

He smiled, but didn't appear satisfied with my answer. Only later, when I had other occasions to talk to him, did his doubt and distrust become comprehensible to me.

There was another puzzling situation which made the psychology of these men a complete riddle for me. Parting from Balthasar, we went into the reading room, and a couple of hours later descended into the corridor of the criminal sector where we met Darcho. It appeared that Balthasar had already told him of our conversation, and had exposed his lie to his face. Darcho seemed to want to avoid the meeting, but I went right up to him and said:

"Hey, why did you tell us that story this morning? I know what really happened."

Without the slightest hesitation, Darcho answered incredulously, as he turned to Benjamin:

"He has gone and told lies to Balthasar, and now he is asking me about them. As if I could have said that I did that job alone? Me? Would I do such a thing?"

He looked at me sadly and went on with a sincerity that astonished me:

"I feel sorry for you."

Even more painful was the verdict in Benjamin's eyes— full of doubt that Darcho could be capable of such a lie. Was it not just as likely that it was I who had lied?

The prisoners were extremely suspicious men; that much was obvious from the very first. This very same Balthasar would later provide not only the explanation but also the accepted "philosophy" of this attitude. He was in my view the archetype of the inmates of the House of Correction, in his outlook, his moral standards, and his life style as a criminal.

Yes, the prisoners were extremely suspicious, men with little faith, and in many of them, as in Balthasar surely, these traits came close to being a disease. And now, while writing this book, I keep wondering:

"What would my prisoner friends think if they read this book? What would Lazki think, and Benjamin, and Hamo, Oss, Yefim Bravelman, Baltho . . .?"

And especially Balthasar, that strong child with a bronze face and iron muscles, the renowned Baltho of the House of Correction.

Evenings in the House of Correction

At seven o'clock the doors of the sector were closed, and the evening activities began in the House of Correction.

Three or four times a week, the prisoners would spend their time in the social center. There might be a play, or a mock trial, or a discussion which would begin with a few brief reports on political, agricultural, medical or not very complicated scientific subjects. The talks were presented by the prisoners, and were often illustrated with pictures drawn by Yefim Bravelman and Belogourov. Questions followed which occasionally erupted into small arguments. Between reports, the prisoners might sing or recite poems; the evenings would usually end with music and dancing.

Once a week or every two weeks, there was a general meeting of the prisoners where discipline and general conduct in the House of Correction were examined. The director of the House always spoke at great length at these meetings. He had a very distinctive style; he heightened his narrative with fables and stories; he involved the prisoners in what he was saying, using them as living illustrations of his thesis. His lectures always provoked heated exchanges in which even Valo, Khouzhan-Khacho, Yefim Bravelman and Balthasar frequently participated. The talks were also given in Turkish and

Russian, or translated for the benefit of those who did not understand Armenian.

Sometimes people were invited from outside to speak to the prisoners on topics that might be of interest to them. I'll never forget the talk we had on chemistry. The cultural committee had invited a professor from the university, who had come prepared to perform experiments with two large boxes of chemicals. The hall was filled with prisoners; still most of them were left outside because of lack of space. The hall was brightly lit; variously shaped tubes, flasks and bottles glistened on the table, producing a magical effect on the prisoners. The speaker was extremely witty, and quickly sensed the psychology of his audience. He focused first on his experiments, and then went on to the explanations. The prisoners seemed most impressed with the experiments that caused an explosion of some kind. Strangely, despite the speaker's very simple language, his explanations were received with considerable skepticism. You would think that they were wary of being deceived or mocked. They tended to be very suspicious anyway; there was nothing in the world they would unquestioningly swallow, as though it were melted butter. Also, the talk seemed more pleasant and comprehensible to them than the actual experiments. You might have expected them to be disappointed with explanations that must have seemed mundane after the magic of the experiments. In any event they were determined to be skeptical, on the one hand to preserve the magic of the illusion, and on the other to confirm their disdain. Their attitude was best exemplified by Lazki who followed the lecture with intent admiration, looking around him uncertainly after every surprising development, for evidences of disbelief that might contradict his own reaction; he did not want to appear to be naively taken in. When he saw the enchantment in everybody's eyes, he felt free to express his own wonder:

"Marvelous."

But after the lecture he told me:

"I don't believe a thing he said; white water turned into red water; and then he left. Let him go and make fools of the city boys."

As for Balthasar:

"Can you insert a chicken's egg in a bottle? Do you want me to tell you how it is done?"

Theater groups came in occasionally to stage small plays and operettas. A young Turkish communist group came frequently, and once even an Armenian choral ensemble, most of whose members were "city girls," in Lazki's words. In that case it was not so much the program that interested the prisoners as, if it may be put in this way, the shape of the performers. The prisoners stared, silently, almost hypnotically, at what seemed to them a miracle unfolding on the stage, at these luminous girls, the sight of their white necks and bare arms enough to stir in them unaccustomed pleasure. Lazki was impatient as usual and leaped on stage during intermission, to sing his own favorite songs. His face had paled and taken on what looked like a spiritual cast; his eyes flowed with the fever of inspiration. The prisoners applauded his performance with fervent appreciation. In one way or another, it was a way of showing those heavenly creatures that we too are human, and have our own natural endowments. Hooray for Lazki! He did not damage our aroused self-esteem before these wondrous beings.

There were days when the cultural activities area was empty; it was then that the unbearable burden of deadly boredom entered the House of Correction and settled in the souls of the prisoners.

On such evenings, a few of the prisoners wandered into the school and reading room, but most of them remained in the cells, where they gathered in small groups. One of them might play on a stringed instrument, while others sat on the cots, legs folded under them, playing dominoes; the backgammon dice clattered; and occasionally the sound of a mandolin or drum echoed through the area. A Kurd on the upper floor, convicted of murder, played the flute. The prisoners gathered around him, drawn by the sad monotone of his music and, in voices that seemed to take refuge in the Kurd's melodies, talked quietly about their families, the friends and enemies they had left behind in the outside world. All the conversations ended with a question someone felt constrained to ask, always disturbing though long since become familiar to everybody.

"I wonder if there will be an amnesty in February?"

Or.

"There's talk about a general amnesty in November. All the prisoners will be released."

No other subject occupied the minds of the prisoners as much as this one, or caused more disputes. Amnesty was the magical word that could offer new life even to a dying prisoner. Anyone going to the city on an errand was inevitably exhorted to learn what he could.

"Find out if there is any talk about amnesty."

And anyone returning from the city would be asked the one question over and over:

"Did you hear anything about an amnesty?"

Amnesty was the center of all their thoughts, the sole source of their hope, the cause of delirious day-dreams—an obsession.

A well known writer[2] had come from abroad to visit me with her engineer companion. I showed them around the House of Correction—the kitchen, the bath, the cells, the cultural activities area, the craft shops. The prisoners showed them the proper respect at all times; when they left, Lazki approached me and in a low expectant voice, asked:

"Where are they from, France?"

"Yes, Lazki, France."

"Did they have any news about an amnesty?"

There were many besides Lazki who came to me with the same question that day.

When there were no plays or other programs, the cultural

affairs area remained open until nine at night. It was possible for prisoners to go and read newspapers in the reading room, exchange books and talk. The legal office would also be open, where prisoners could get help in filling out applications to various factories, and for whatever other counsel they might need. Rehearsals would be going on in the hall, the group on duty would be clearing out the school, and the production shop of the artistic area, located in the cultural activities section, would be in full operation.

It is there that the prisoners made frames, small boxes, and other articles of wood, which they put on sale every Sunday in the city. Warm, brightly lit, the shops were pleasant to enter in the evening; it was pleasant to listen to the intimate songs of the thin saws, and watch the varied forms emerge from the wood, while others stood ready to polish or assemble with nails or glue. Belogourov and Yefim Bravelman painted scenes on the frames, the former almost always working on seascapes, while the latter's preference was for village scenes on winter nights—snow, fire, a small hut, with a warm light shining through the window, and above, a yellow half-moon through the white clouds.

A pale young man named Mischa, a drug addict, worked in the shop. Convicted for robbery, he had been in prison before. He said he was from Persia, was Armenian, but spoke only Russian. He had delicate features, straight blond hair, and blue eyes. In spite of his frail appearance, he was able to down a teacup full of straight alcohol with no difficulty whatever. He was a decent young man, and seemed able to do everything. He could paint, play almost every instrument, mold little deers from the dough, make frames out of wood. Sometimes in the evening, he would pick up a guitar from the cultural activities section and entertain us with Russian, Ukrainian, and Georgian songs, or with some sad or lively popular tunes. We would be in the shop where the work seemed to halt almost on cue. With the entertainment going so well, and the audience raptly attentive, Yefim Bravelman would quickly join in with his own songs, followed by Benjamin's dance tunes on the violin. The prisoners danced; then the music and noise stopped, and work was resumed in the shop.

It was when we were gathered in the shop on such evenings, singing and dancing, that Belogourov, a cryptic smile on his face, would suddenly come up to me and embark on tales about Yefim Bravelman's wicked deeds. I knew that the things he said about Yefim had to be true, but I did not like being an audience for such recitals. Belogourov was a melancholy man; nature had given him sad eyes and a sour disposition.

After the cultural activities area closed, the prisoners retired to their cells; there was time there for small games, conversation, and music; for some it was time for surrender to daydreams and boredom. Souren's friend Khachig, a romantic young man in his mid-twenties, paced the corridor like a caged beast, his hands flung behind him, head bent in a posture of despair. I walked along with him frequently.

"Eh, Khachig, what are you thinking about?"

"Ah, Comrade Charents, what else can I be thinking of?" he would answer, without missing a step. "No amnesty yet, so we can go about the business of our lives."

"It will come, don't worry; we'll be freed next November."

"Where is it? That wretched thing hasn't come." It was always the same answer, the only suitable accompaniment to his restless pacing that ended when he got sleepy and had to lie down.

In spite of his restlessness, Khachig was calm and eventempered, like his friends Souren and Nicol. I was told they had been convicted of burglary, but I didn't know any particulars of the crime. One evening when Khachig was pacing back and forth in the corridor in his usual manner, I went up to him once more, as I had done on many other occasions.

"Eh, Khachig, you're at it again."

"What else am I to do? If the amnesty ever came, I could go about my business."

He stopped unexpectedly and looked straight at me.

"Will there really be a general amnesty next year?"

"Yes, Khachig. I'm sure you'll be freed."

He smiled and shook his head sadly.

"I'm afraid they won't free us. There have been two amnesties since we were convicted, and they never let us go."

"Why, Khachig?"

"Oh, damn the luck. It happened that we killed Turks, both times. It became a national issue. At first they wanted to execute us, but the Central Committee changed that."

I learned more about it later. There were apparently four of them who had made a practice of robbing Turkish homes; and two of the robberies ended with murder being committed. But they gave up crime altogether after a few attempts, and got regular jobs. For two years they lived normal lives, harmed nobody. But by some accident of fate, their crimes were discovered and they were sent to the House of Correction— Souren, Nicol, Khachig, and another whom I did not know because he died in the hospital two months before I arrived. They used to say that the dead one, the legendary Mesrob, had been their leader. They told stories about his strength, character, "courage."

Although I lived in the hospital, I always spent the evenings in the cells of the criminal sector, in part to observe how the prisoners managed, and in part to escape the suffocation of loneliness and boredom. And no matter when I entered the criminal sector, the picture was always the same: games, conversation, music. I don't know why the sounds of the sector, the nocturnal buzzing of the cells, saddened me. The people seemed unreal, fantastic; the entire place a delirious fabrication. With all my being I felt that the men who were singing, laughing, arguing, playing music, dejected and forlorn, as much as the creature called man can be. And it was so. And the proof? The prisoners became extremely irritable in the evening; they seemed disturbed, on edge, fighting for things that hardly mattered, hurting and mocking each other with words. The limitless human soul was rebelling, demanding freedom and more space, space to spread out and move around in, to take walks in the streets and fields, to see friends and enemies for opportunities to embrace or fight. And they resorted to whatever means they could, even to the most unlikely pretexts, to suppress that unbearable spiritual ache, that inescapable depression.

And what better way was there for them to relieve the accumulated pressures that drew their nerves taut than to mock, vilify, and belittle others. One way or another, you can take your resentment out on someone else, whoever he may be, close comrade or stranger, and take whatever relief it might offer. So it should not be surprising that the prisoners sometimes, often even, behaved in ways that were not easy to rationalize.

One evening I had gone to the cells on the upper floor. In the eighth cell, I saw that Balthasar had made a hospital gown out of a sheet and draped himself with it, fastening it here and there with pins; there was an assortment of papers under his arm as he stood so strangely attired in the middle of the cell. The prisoners were laughing and giving advice about how to look even more like a real doctor. When all his preparations were completed, he approached me and said cryptically:

"Come with us. It will be very interesting."

Then he went out quickly, all the prisoners trailing after him. I noticed that one of them had a container of water hidden under his jacket. The procession hurried down the corridor and into the last cell. Balthasar was the first to go in, with brisk, authoritative steps; three prisoners were behind him while the others stood outside the door.

"Who is the senior in this cell?" Balthasar asked with a dry, official cough. A man came forward.

"Are there any new prisoners here?"

"Two."

"Who are the new ones?"

The senior prisoner pointed to them. They had already taken off their clothes and gone to bed. They were peasants.

"Wake them up. Tell them the doctor has come to examine them."

The senior prisoner and his cellmates looked at each other and smiled, but offered no objections. It was obviously not the first time that they had witnessed such a charade, and they were anticipating the pleasure of what was to come.

When the senior woke the newcomers and told them that the doctor was there to examine them, they rubbed their eyes and jumped to their feet. They approached Balthasar hesitantly, watching him with animal curiosity.

At that moment one of our group approached Balthasar and handed him a paper.

"Comrade Doctor," he said with a trembling voice, "please do not refuse my request."

"This is not the time; later," Balthasar reprimanded him. but he took the paper and pretended to read it.

"All right, I will have you hospitalized tomorrow."

All this, as had been calculated, made the necessary impression on the newcomers. They could hardly doubt that this was indeed the doctor who had come to examine them. And who knows how great his authority may be?

Balthasar told the first of the new prisoners:

"Uncover your chest."

The prisoner obeyed. Balthasar put his ear to the man's chest, as if to listen.

"Good, now your back."

The man turned around and pulled up his shirt. All the others were trying desperately to keep from exploding with laughter. They watched intently as Balthasar tapped the man's back several times with the end of a pencil.

"All right. Now lower these."

He pointed to the trousers. The man obediently lowered

his trousers, and just as he did the prisoner who had brought the container of water slipped up beside Balthasar and splashed the man's exposed body. The man immediately pulled up his trousers.

Everybody was shaking with laughter. Balthasar tweaked the man's nose with contempt, as though to emphasize the wretched deception they had perpetrated.

This is the kind of thing they were driven to for some diversion, to dissipate the monotony of empty evenings, when there were no organized programs in the cultural activities area.

Then it was back to the cells once more, and to bed one after the other, with sleep eventually settling on their restless, desperate hearts, to be transported in their dreams perhaps to that world beyond the gates and walls of the House of Correction.

In the criminal sector, to which I was later transferred, I noticed that many of the prisoners were restless in their sleep as well, talking, moving, cursing, smiling. As far as I could remember, Dostoevsky wrote about this too.

But no relief was to be found in sleep. I was deeply disturbed by this in the beginning. As I lay awake, I could observe the men around me, asleep, but talking, smiling, sometimes screaming. The young peasant nearest me would shake his arms in his sleep, make threatening gestures, and wrestle with invisible enemies who were as far away from him, as the liberating dawn seemed to me.

The Last Days

My last days in the Erevan House of Correction seemed like a wild nightmare. What kind of thoughts can spark the mind of a man who had, for one reason or another, been trapped in a place like this, shut in by four walls, forced to live among derelicts and criminals, while not too far off he can make out the tombstones of the cemetery, where under a small mound lie the remains of the person he loved the most, his wife? Who could for very long enjoy the slightest measure of contentment, or tolerate any pleasant thoughts in such personal circumstances?

Still some faces, some events, some incidents which I will never forget, emerge from the turmoil of my last days in the House of Correction. I want to set down some of these in the last part of my memoirs.

A few days before my release, while I was pacing the corridor of the criminal sector, the immense figure of Uncle Aslan suddenly loomed before me. He was, if you recall, the old bandit who had taken to the mountains because of his great love for his wife, and for a few years was involved in many daring escapades before being caught and confined in the House of Correction, where the peasant bandit had turned to writing. Old and gentle now, he had been pardoned by the Central Committee.

"Comrade Charents, I have a request to make of you," Uncle Aslan said, smiling in his uncertain way.

"What is it, Uncle Aslan?"

I noticed he was holding a few notebooks in his hand, at which he kept glancing nervously.

"I am an old man," he went on. "I have no family, no one at all. I'm alone in the world. And all I have is this. This is my only legacy." And Uncle Aslan handed me his notebooks.

"I have written my story, all of it, everything there is. Please take this and keep it, so Uncle Aslan's name doesn't vanish from the world. There is just me and this, no wealth, no heirs, nothing else."

I looked at him and saw that tears had moistened his eyes. Even as he was about to be released, he seemed sad; the old bandit was dark as death.

"All right, Uncle Aslan, give it to me. I'll see that it's kept."
He gave me the books. There were six notebooks, a bit worn,
with yellow covers, all filled with dense, crooked, delicate
script, which recalled the letters of a child just beginning to
learn how to write.

"I thank you very much," Uncle Aslan said.

He shook my hand, looked longingly at his notebooks for
the last time, and left.

I turned over the notebooks of Uncle Aslan's life story
to the cultural affairs sector of the House of Correction. If any
of you ever find yourself there, you can visit the cultural sec-
tor and see Uncle Aslan's yellowed, frayed notebooks, with
their child's script.

It was in those days too that Souren, that thin pale youth
and friend of Nicol and Khachig, once sought me out in the
yard. A shy smile on his face, he too handed me a thin
notebook and, looking away from me, said:

"This is my play. I have written it here. If you have the
time, read it."

And without waiting for an answer, he went away.

It was a student's pad, with a blue cover, ten to twelve
pages in all. The title of the play was inscribed on the cover,
along with the name of the author. I began to read. There were
two characters, Friedrich and Franz, two thieves who, as the
play began, were reproaching each other for not being
trustworthy friends, for betraying each other. Soon it became
clear that they had committed a successful robbery and
couldn't decide how to divide the loot in a way that would
satisfy both. The play ended with them poisoning each other.
In justice to Souren, it must be added that the dialogue was
fluent and believable, though that might have been because
Souren was himself sufficiently familiar with the thought pat-
terns of his criminal characters.

Nevertheless, the pale youth with the pale notebook left
a pleasant, even lyrical impression on me. It is difficult to forget
the face of that morphine addict and his notebook in which

a pair of thieves ended by killing each other.

Two days after he gave me the book, Souren approached me again, but not to ask about the play.

"Comrade Charents," he said, eyes always shyly averted, "I have a request. Please do not refuse me."

"What is it, Souren?"

"Please ask the chief to allow me and Khachig to go to Etchmiadzin to work with Nicol. We want to go there to learn a trade."

"All right, I'll ask. I think he'll let you, if you promise to behave yourselves."

"What are you saying, Comrade Charents?" He was sad and serious. "If we remain here, what will become of us? I want to learn a craft, and go to Leninakan after my release, and get a decent job. I will take my mother with me, and we'll live together."

There was anxiety and regret on his pale face as he spoke, the kind of confusion young tuberculars radiate, sitting on the balcony of a sanatorium, dreaming of warmth and life, of the sun and singing girls in the spring.

A few days later Souren and Khachig went to Etchmiadzin, where some of our prisoners were assigned. Soon news came back to us that they were making progress in their work.

A prisoner named Kourken visited our cell frequently during those last days. He was from Leninakan, a real Kumretsi, always drunk, but a master goldsmith.

In the House of Correction he had a goldsmith's shop where he worked all the time. He was convicted in an accidental homicide and sentenced to prison. I don't know why, but I got to like him immediately. Raised in the joyous, friendly tradition of Kumri,[3] he was a gregarious, hard-working man who had met with misfortune because of his drinking. He was in his early thirties, of medium height, his face toughened by his work, his hair clipped short. He had an original, picturesque way of speaking and telling a story.

One evening, while we were sitting around talking, one of

the prisoners, whose child had just died in the village, said that he would return to that village when he was released, and have the grave opened, and look on his child a last time to satisfy his yearning.

"Don't do it, even if your life depends on it," Kourken exclaimed with fear, as he jumped up from his place. "It will be so terrifying, you will never get over it."

"Why?"

"Why else? That's what happened to me when my father died. I loved him very much. He was the most precious thing in the world to me. Once I got drunk, and opened the grave. After that, it turned into an obsession, and I couldn't get away from it. This is the kind of love it is, love of the dead. At night I would go to the cemetery, I would sleep there. I would open the grave and look at it. Do you know what it is like?"

"What?"

"If you open the grave weeks after the death, there will be something like a white web spread over the body. You will have to remove it to see the face, and the face will be festered, and there might be water in the grave. But I had such a longing to look that nothing could help me. If I missed it for two days, I would be frantic. My friends and I would go to the cemetery with drums and flute. I would open it and cry. Finally it was enough, I thought; I had to stop. So I had a tombstone placed on it, but even that didn't help. I began to dig from the side. One time I wanted to move the head a bit forward; it snapped off in my hand. I took it out and placed it on the stone. From inside—do you know what pomegranate seeds look like?—tiny red worms tumbled out, just like pomegranate seeds. They are the worms that eat the dead."

We stared at Kourken, repelled by his nightmarish story. We are accustomed to picturing the dead, especially our loved ones, as disembodied and sanctified, just as they existed in our memory. Even in their coffins, they are seen as peacefully asleep, sullen or smiling, the serene sadness of farewell, or the nostalgic smile of departure. It was this sacred predisposition that the excited Kourken was offending with the awful realism of his experiences, leaving us all extremely depressed.

I could not sleep that night, and wandered restlessly along the upper corridor of the criminal sector till dawn. Life, the world, sky and sun, whatever is bright and beautiful in this transitory life of ours, seemed to me pallid and dreadful, with my mind settling under "the web" which had spread over it, along with the ravenous red worms that looked like "pomegranate seeds."

The last memory of those days is of the mischievous "rascals," with shiny black eyes and faces burnished by the cold, little "hooligans" our chief had picked up one evening, put in his car and brought to the House of Correction. When I went to see them, they were already asleep in his office, near the stove; their small, dirty, but rather gentle faces already radiated the comfort they had escaped into from the cold street.

These "hooligans" brought a great deal of happiness to the inmates of the House of Correction. All three, eight to ten years old, but daring and bright, and already with considerable experience, would of course have become thieves and convicts if they remained in the street. They were the "successors" of Valo, Khouzhan-Khatcho, Macho and Hussein, "recruits" ready to fill the ranks of the criminal world.

When I saw them again in the morning, I asked:

"Do you have any idea what kind of place you are in?"

Two of them, grinning derisively like men of the world, smirked, and the youngest one answered:

"A saloon."

They were given new clothes and transferred to the pig farm of the House of Correction which was opposite our building. Anoush and Marguerite worked on some old prisoners' garments during the nights, and made some ridiculous make-shift clothes for them to wear. They were given one corner of the servants' quarters, and seemed content with their fate. The chief tried to get them admitted to the children's center, but the matter was repeatedly delayed. I left those three small "hooligans" there, three little friends of my last days in the House of Correction, three little brothers.

[1] According to the memoirs of M. Gorky and N. Krupskaya.
[2] Reference is to Zabelle Yessayan.
[3] An earlier name for Leninakan.

Essays & Diary

The "Declaration of the Three" reflects Charents' reactions to the literary environment of the 1920s. He was later to repudiate the basic positions set forth in the manifesto. "On the Boundary of Two Worlds," written on the death of Hovhaness Toumanian, projects Charents' conception of what Armenian literature was before the Russian Revolution, and what it should be in his time. "The Deceased Gentleman" is a thinly disguised imaginative assessment of the political events of the immediate past. It is a long dialogue ostensibly between him and Vahan Navasardian, a prominent Dashnagtsagan leader and used by Charents as a representation of the party, which Charents assumed to have been buried in 1920 with the fall of the Republic and the Sovietization of Armenia. It is a cleverly devised dialogue with evenly matched protagonists, equally eloquent in the defense of their respective political beliefs. It might be wondered whether Charents really intended to ridicule the party that was forced to surrender power, or whether he sought to provide readers in Armenia with a fleeting glimpse of opinion prevalent abroad. The latter possibility may be far-fetched, but is suggested by the forceful articulation of the antagonistic views.

Only a few diary entries have survived (perhaps there were no others), but offer their special insights, particularly with respect to individuals like the political leader Alexander Miasnikian and the poet Vahan Derian, as well as the literary scene in the Soviet Union. He found the latter rather bleak, citing Maxim Gorky as the only author who wrote what he wanted to. Charents was prophetic when he mused on what a terrible gap Gorky's death would leave.

Much of Charents' work—possibly including other diary entries— written after 1934, was dispersed among various individuals. The painter Regina Ghazarian, for example, only a young girl in 1937, at great risk to her own life, kept some of the most powerful of Charents' poems. Some were actually buried and brought to light some thirty years later, a few pages already turned to dust, others still intact or only partially destroyed. Some may still be locked in official archives. These may shed valuable light on the poet's thoughts and feelings in his last days. Among the surviving papers there is a four-verse segment of a poem dedicated to Stalin, entitled "The Third Dawn," written in 1936 on the proclamation of Stalin's constitution. But there were others in which he plainly attacked Stalin. Various explanations of this apparently equivocal attitude have been suggested. The authorship of the first poem may be questioned; or if he did write it, his state of mind at the time. The clearest evidence with regard to his attitude on Stalin and his regime may derive from his arrest in 1937. The critic Hrant Tamrazian, writing about that time in Charents' life, asserts that "from what we can adduce, he had the chance to save himself with some compromise," probably referring to the statement by the Chekist interrogator of Armenian writers, Valery Kirpotin, who had told Charents directly (Pakin Literary Monthly, No. 3, March 1985, Beirut, Lebanon):

"The road for redemption for Charents is not closed," implying that he might yet recant and save his neck. The miserable Chekist did not understand that while Charents might conceivably compromise himself, he would not compromise his literary heritage. Charents' spiritual antecedents, Siamanto, Varoujan, and Roupen Sevag had faced comparable challenges and had not faltered. It was not for Charents to betray their moral legacy. Kirpotin was wrong. All roads, in spite of the temptations, were irrevocably closed.

"On the Boundary of Two Worlds"[1]

> How much will you be tormented still
> On the boundary of two worlds . . .
> —*Vahan Derian*[2]

Hovhaness Toumanian.

It was not about his life and achievements that I felt impelled to write when I received the news of his death. Whatever might be said of the high artistic quality of his work has already been said. The public relevance and social character of his writing have long since been demonstrated.[3] Little that is new remains to be discussed by critics yet to come and, if that "little" is to be explored at all, it will have to be as the result of long and arduous research by specialists. Rather, it was my wish to set down in the issue of the journal[4] dedicated to his memory some thoughts and reminiscences about our poetry in the past, which were evoked by the image of Toumanian's passing from us. When the "past" is spoken of now, it can only refer to everything prior to October 1917. The sharp sword of the proletarian revolution drew a red line through that terrifying time, and whatever remained on *that* side of the line became the ancient past for those standing on *this* side, a past that was distant and unintelligible, the reflection of dark years, the haziness of centuries. The line deepened further in the course of five tumultuous years, becoming an impassable abyss—and there were people who were left dangling on that forbidding boundary that divided two worlds.

Of those left on that "boundary of two worlds," the greatest and most tragic figure was Vahan Derian, the "last poet"[5] of our old, pre-October literature, who had one foot in the old while reaching for the new with the other. He wanted to cross the boundary, but did not, remaining imprisoned in the abyss, like "Jesus nailed to his cross."[6]

The meager pages of our poetry are a three-ply chain that stretches from the dark times of our past to the present, toward

October. On this end of the chain, the closest to us and the dearest was Derian; on the other end, actually the beginning of the modern era, was Toumanian. And between them was Avetik Issahakian, close to both, to the left of one and to the right of the other.

The first to go was the youngest, Derian, who was more nearly part of us. With his death we lost that element of our poetic past which longed for identification with us, while it sustained its relationship with the old, with Issahakian and Toumanian.

The greatest of them is going to his eternal rest now, the patriarch, the great master of modern Armenian poetry, Hovhaness Toumanian. Only Issahakian survives, orphaned now on both left and right. The sole survivor of the old now who, settled in Berlin,[7] dreams of his native beginnings, the phantoms of Alakiaz, and eternal love. He does not know, he does not seem to sense that this world no longer exists, that it has vanished, turned into mist and memory. There are countless others too who are similarly unaware, or are reluctant to acknowledge that bitter truth; but a stern and merciless time, soaring beyond their reach, is indifferent to their "predilections."

Those three brightest stars of the poetry of our recent past are, of course, all very dear to us. Still, I do not feel it would be unbecoming or futile to look back on all three simply to appreciate what we have lost with Toumanian's death, to determine the voice of what world was silenced with Derian's lyre, and to make out what Issahakian continues to murmur to this day.

It would assuredly not be futile, particularly since it would reveal once more how much life has changed, how great the distance has become between us, and how difficult it is for us, for those who follow them, to "continue" their work, as so many are naively "advising" us to do. And perhaps this review will indicate why our interest, the interest of the "new" poets, is veering toward the horizons of other literatures where, particularly in the Russian, it is seeking the paths and directions of our poetry of tomorrow.

In plain language, it is my purpose to probe for a moment the depths of their creativity; may they forgive me for these words which are set down with affection and admiration, though some may view them as ill-timed and gratuitous.

Hovhaness Toumanian lived among us, but was somehow removed from us. He seemed to me often as though in a dream, or an enchanted mirror slipped into our world from a children's fable; whoever looks into it sees his own childhood, dark and irretrievable. Toumanian was the living mirror of the old, of the past, of the obscure and magical life of our patriarchal villages. He illuminated the years that had become smoke and fog. He sat in a trolley, in his European clothes and velvet hat, going from street to street or, the pain of his patriarchal consciousness creasing his face, gazing at the airplanes soaring over the vast city—while the old, the past, occupied his soul—Loretsi Sako, Anoush, the love songs of the mountains, the night of the Ascension, the primitive love and hatred of the "brave boys," Mossi and Saro.[8]

It was in an apartment furnished in Western style, the light of the electric bulb cold and unfriendly, even the landlord's hospitality seeming so strange, that Loretsi Hovhaness, attired in his European clothes, for years composed his simple and endearing songs for us, dark and mysterious poems in which his patriarchal soul surged toward the world of his fathers. His imagination was brilliant and clear, like an enchanted mirror, or the waters of a fabulous stream, reflecting images and scenes from the past. Wherever he went, Brother Karnig would rise to find the fortune he dreamed of, wondrous and regal, after having vanquished the wicked. To be worthy of such kingly fortune, the braves of Parvana flew from the semi-darkness of the poet's secluded room, from the heart of the poet himself, to all regions of the world, to seek the eternal flame. The black-eyed mistress of Temook fortress would leave the national castle of Nadir Shah, bewitched by the curse of the old shrew of a mother-in-law, flying out of the window, transformed into a lapwing. The "wicked" would oppress Tamar, while her lover drowned in the "joyous sea of Van," so that the island might be called "Akhtamar." Fable, the mist of vanished years, the haziness of centuries.

He was a wizard, busy resurrecting the past in the age of steam and electricity. In a terrifying time of world wars and revolutionary eruptions, this Loretsi Hovhaness was a wondrous revelation, a genius, impossible and unbelievable.

Sometimes he seemed to become child-like, writing simple and unpretentious songs, poems, and fables—seemingly for other children. And in these songs too, the old, the patriarchal, and the magical were evoked. He knew all the birds and animals, understood their language, knew their habits, their way of life. They were part of his life, like the lark nestling "in the Loree fields,"[9] waiting for him to pass. He shot a bird once and all his life it seemed to him that "it was still flying in his mind, its wings bloody and broken."[10] And sometimes, abruptly aware of being in an unknown, foreign place, the Loretsi wizard was saddened, tears filling his eyes, suddenly a stranger in his time. The poet's heart grieved then and, with a voice seemingly drawn from the cemetery, he called forth the old, the distant, the unreturnable.

Come back,
Back to the flooding river of spring,
Days that are past, love and joy,
Return, come back together.

And if they came, what would it matter?

But can we really wonder why childhood is so deeply cherished? No matter how dark and difficult, it is a kind of supernatural music. Toumanian was the seductive lyricist of our irretrievable childhood, emerging from the swaddling clothes of our public life, in the days when he was still a school teacher, a village intellectual newly arrived in the city—he, Ghazaros Aghayan, Broshian, and others. The others passed on, became memories of the time, and left Loretsi Hovhaness alone. Was it perhaps they whom the orphaned poet, arrived in a new era, was calling back with such compelling nostalgia?

Two literary generations had passed before his eyes; Issahakian had matured; and Derian had emerged from adolescent constraints, created a body of work, and died. He remained, still alert and wise, Loretsi Hovhaness, the last Mohican of the patriarchal era of our poetry, the last wizard of our lyric art, and he departs from us today.

Next was Issahakian, a successor, however, who had lived and worked in full view of his predecessor, who was both friend and contemporary, and at the same time removed from him by a generation, and with altogether different origins. He was not from a village, as was Loretsi Hovhaness, but from a town of small shopkeepers. Strong and vigorous, Kumretsi[12] Avo had achieved public recognition at about the same time as Toumanian, with his renowned "Songs and Wounds."[13] He had come out of Kumri, a town of craftsmen, and brought with him the lively songs, the mixed emotions and experiences of its "fraternal youth." It was an intellectual emerging from a community of small artisans, who succeeded the patriarchal, primitive peasant, though not yet forgetting the village, remaining a stranger to the city, fearing it in fact, and recoiling from the terror of its inevitable triumph, keeping his eyes always on the village, pining for his garden on the banks of the Arax, where he could absorb the warmth of the girl he loved, Shoushan. Kumretsi Avo was the poet of the small craftsmen disturbed by the capitalism newly established in our land; and the younger brother of Loretsi Hovhaness; and between them lies an entire generation which saw the small craftsmen succeed the patriarchal peasant.

The world was a bitter place for him. The past, the village which he had left hungry and impoverished, was a paradise beside the unimaginable horrors to come, a dream world of fables and fairies. Wavering betweeen village and city, between what was and what was to be, deprived of a steadying class perspective, the artist "made bitter judgments and did nothing."[14] His protests were not directed against anything specific, but against the "unfeeling world" generally, rebelling against it from time to time, cursing, getting drunk, and otherwise evincing a personal alienation. Separated from Kumri and its craftsmen and comrades, Avo went to Europe where he came into contact with famed philosophers and sages, from whom he derived one thing—which even without them should surely have been evident—the insight that "man is a beast to man," that it is better to go among beasts than to remain in the family of "man."[15]

As it was, time was passing and new intellectuals were emerging from the large cities identified with the bourgeois way of life; their poet was from Akhalkalak, from the village, but one who had grown up in Moscow. He was already closer to Kumretsi Avo than to Loretsi Hovhaness; 17 years younger than the latter, in fact, and two generations removed.

Vahan Derian.

He had inhaled the damp air of the great capitalist metropolis, had become a sensitive poet, imbued with that city's bourgeois culture. To Akhalkalaktsi Vahan, the village had become a "fantasy," about which, if he were to show any interest at all, he could write no more than "stylized gallantries." His insecure financial circumstances, the absence of a strong tie with the class whose culture he had fully absorbed and accepted, would cause despair and frustration, and drive him into new directions. Like his elder brother, Kumretsi Avo, Derian was not indifferent to the life of the big city; he was conscious of the clash of its diverse elements, and he realized that his sympathies should be with the lower classes; but with an education that linked him firmly to bourgeois culture, he was left immobilized, as he had said plaintively, "on the boundary of two worlds." He fought and struggled in the front rank of the political revolution, but in his heart the old prevailed, the customs and the culture of the enemy army,[16] Briussov, Blok, and the gazelles of Viacheslav Ivanov.

There on the boundary of two worlds, he was tormented without consolation and, still uprooted, died like an aristocrat-soldier, dedicated to the deliverance of the proletariat; his tragic death shattered the chain that linked old and new, leaving Kumretsi Avo one generation off, and Loretsi Hovhaness still another generation beyond. It is the panorama of our public life seen through the prism of our poetry; it is the lyricized epitome of our pre-revolutionary life.

From Hovhaness Toumanian to Vahan Derian.

It is like going from Pushkin to Blok to Bailmont.

Only after making this comparison does the astonishing absurdity of their having been contemporaries become apparent. Can you picture Pushkin together with Bailmont and Briussov in the streets of Moscow today?

That is how it was with us.

That is how it is in economically backward countries where beside the remnants of the ancestral village are centers of industry, like Tiflis and Baku; and between the two loom three centuries of time (in our Russian life at least), and perhaps even more.

From these ancestral villages, including the petty bourgeois craft towns, to our great contemporary cities, runs the line of progress in our life.

These memories and feelings were stirred in me by the sad news of his death, shaping distant and intimate images out of the mist of years[17]—images of Loretsi Hovhaness, Kumretsi Avo, and Akhalkalaktsi Vahan, distant though dear, easing the pain in my heart. And once again I understood and felt how close they are to me, and at the same time so far removed.

Distant, impalpable, they are like shadows sliding out of the past. Childhood and adolescence are the same for us, far out of reach; whatever no longer exists has become memory, mist and memory.

An abyss opened between us yesterday separating us forever from everything on the other side, turned now into dream and delirium. And we know that any attempt to bridge the chasm can only serve to revive the old, whatever has already gone beyond our reach, and unsettle the dust of years. We, *the new*, stand on this side of the boundary; beyond lies the old, distant and dream-like, even if still recognized and cherished.

These days have made a different sound echo in our hearts, the sound of Moscow and Baku and the big industrial centers which, while they may not be part of the traditional "Erkir Nayiri," are closer to us, tied more intimately to our life and future than Sevan or ancient Etchmiadzin.

Whoever has heard the roar of October, for him the world has already shrunk into a "small, small street";[18] and it is possible for a Ching-Fu to greet him from far-off Peking; or a Hans; or a Boghos. Our life has surged beyond the narrow Nayirian circle and become a part of the progress of the world, whereas our Nayirian way of life remains pre-industrial. This can only mean that the poetry that reaches for the future, for the dynamic music of the time, must draw its inspiration from the life of those centers; otherwise it will be left dangling in mid-air, somewhere "on the boundary of two worlds," where Derian remained. What is to come is the industrial, the dynamic, the electrifying, that which

> *shall come, shall come, shall come!*
> *With the powerful ringing of iron . . .*
> *toward our stone huts,*
> *toward our wretched country.*[19]

This is what is to come, what has already entered our lives, already edged into Erevan and Kumri. And it will decide whether our country is to be or is not to be, and it will require a new language to define its social character, its new creative impulses. The songs of this time must be different and, even if it were desirable, they could not possibly be connected with the old. Perhaps our poetry too will quiver a long time "on the boundary between two worlds." But the quivering will be from creative labor pains, and not from agony. Our poetry of tomorrow will rise like a superstructure barely able to keep up with the growth of the country. There is no other path for its development. And our new poets will be as far from the cherished ways of Toumanian, Issahakian, and Derian, as dear as they may be to us. It is only through the rejection of their world that the old poets can be accepted and honored by the new. Otherwise it will be a regression into the mist of the centuries, into a death-like delirium.

Welcome to the bright future; eternal rest and reverence for the worthy poets of the past. Before Hovhaness Toumanian's tomb, let this be our one wish:

May our existence, and therefore our poetry, not waver long "on the boundary of two worlds." May the life we seek be realized quickly when, as the last and senior poet of the past devoutly desired, the "children" will be able to live, but not "as we did."[20]

[1] First published in "Soviet Armenia," April 3, 1923.
[2] From the Derian poem that begins with the line, "Yet how much moaning, how much grief."
[3] Reference is to P. Makintsian's article, "Hovh. Toumanian," published in "Karoun" Almanach, Moscow, 1912; and A. Mardouni's (A. Miasnikian) book, "The Social Value of Hovh. Toumanian's Work," published in Tiflis, 1923.
[4] The April 3, 1923 issue of "Soviet Armenia" was dedicated to Toumanian's memory.
[5] Reference is to Derian's poem beginning with, "Am I the last poet?"
[6] Reference unknown.
[7] Charents' information is wrong. Issahakian was in Venice in 1923. He was misled by an inaccurate report published in "Baku" (No. 6-7, 1923), placing Issahakian in Berlin.
[8] References are to characters and themes in Toumanian's work.
[9] From a Toumanian quatrain that begins with the line, "In the clouds and snow of autumn."
[10] From a Toumanian quatrain that begins: "I shot a bird one day."
[11] A Toumanian quatrain.
[12] Kumretsi: someone from Kumri, later Alexandropol, now Leninakan.
[13] Issahakian's first volume of poems, Alexandropol, 1897.
[14] From Issahakian's poem, beginning: "Ah, our heart full of pain, grief."

[15] Charents has paraphrased a couplet from Issahakian's "Abou Lala Mahari."

[16] Charents pictures symbolism in that light, deriding it as a literary movement.

[17] This is a literal use of a sentence from the Charents novel, *Erkir Nayiri*.

[18] A line from Charents' "Poem for All."

[19] From the Charents volume, "Poesozourna."

[20] The final line of Toumanian's poem, "Last Blessing."

Pages from the Diary (1934)

March 14, 1934

It is almost a year now since, through Khanjian's arrangement, I withdrew Vahan Derian's manuscripts[1] from the literary museum for the purpose of preparing his unpublished works for publication. I have begun copying the manuscripts to have them at hand always and to protect the originals from the damage of frequent leafing. I have not yet finished, nor am I rushing either. Every time I remember that there in the drawer of my study are Derian's manuscripts—think of it, his very own manuscripts, pages written by his hand—I have a strangely tender and pleasant sensation. Whenever I am depressed, I take them out and look at them. It is as if I have secreted the sun in my desk drawer. Those silky sheets, covered with black India ink, shaped into noble miraculous letters. The man had an extraordinarily legible hand, and delicate, like all his creative work, delicate and precise. This is the greatest joy of my life, to pick up these manuscripts and look at them every now and then.

"Oh, my distant friend, Oh, Vahan Derian."[2]

Among our young writers, I like Armen[3] the best. He seems the most original and serious figure in our new literature. I remember his arrival in Erevan.[4] It was in 1926; K. Mahari[5] brought him to me. The first work of his that I read was astonishing; none of our new writers has been as original as Armen in his very first steps. And his treatment is characteristic of our literary climate. Not only was he not recognized then for his exceptional power, he has not been recognized to this day.

March 18

Of all the men I have met, the one who has left the greatest impression on me is A. Miasnikian.[6] His appearance was in itself forceful and striking. Of all the descriptions that have occurred to me, the one that seems to fit him best is, "cast in bronze," which I have applied to him in my poems. Not his imposing face alone, but his entire being seemed to be made of bronze, projecting an image of complete self-sufficiency and self-control. The eyes were dominant, a deep hazel, the whites with a greyish shade, his glance exerting an almost physical impact. Few could withstand the power of that glance, and refrain from lowering their eyes under its hypnotic pressure.

I have seen Derian only once, in Tiflis, in 1917,[7] I think, in a teahouse then on Kalavin Street.[8] He was sitting with someone sipping tea and reading the paper. Kara-Darvish, the only Armenian writer then known to me, approached him. I envied him the experience of talking to such a genius. For me then, Derian was not only a great poet, but also a mystical personality. Soon he got up, went to the coatrack near the door, put on his coat (the color of a mouse, the kind of coat worn by travelers at that time), stuffed the paper in his pocket and left. I went out into the street and looked after him for a long time. His dark, lightly yellowish, very Armenian face, and the damp look of his eyes, remained fixed in my mind. There seemed to be a mist hanging over his face which his eyes had to penetrate. Though his face, with some coarse lines, was Armenian, it reflected a delicate refinement, and intellectual preoccupation. There was the stamp of a frail weariness on his face, and his appearance corresponded completely with his poetry.

I did not see him again.

March 19

In the collection called *Mankind*, what is seen as "tragedy" can have meaning only so long as people view their lives as personal and uniquely individual. The death of a particular person is a tragedy for me because I see him as altogether unique. But if you were to look at this with a skeptical eye, thinking, "What is it to me if your loved one has died?", the idea of "tragedy" ends, and the idea of human life as "calendar" begins.

"You, yesterday; I, today; and tomorrow, he."[9]

But is the idea of "calendar" enough for human life?

If it were, not only would art be useless, but also science, and everything linked to the tradition of being.

Sometimes, after writing what I think is a good poem, I reflect:

"Let us allow for a moment that this poem is more successful than any ever written by our greatest poets. But can this one then have that same meaning? Of course not. Why?

Answer this question for yourself, dear reader.

At present, in the entire Soviet Union, the only writer who has not lost his distinctive literary style and his own unique characteristics, and writes about everything with his own words, and not in the stereotype of an "ideological style," is Maxim Gorky. He can, for example, write a preface about any author, and not feel constrained to refer to any attitudes on class. Also he can—it is a sublime prerogative—talk about poetry the way one generally talks about it, praising the spiritual pleasure of creativity, the natural and the human, love and the humanitarian impulses in literature. In this respect, Gorky's introductions for Stepan Zweig and Mikhail Prishvin are wondrously unique in all of Soviet publishing. One reads those introductions with admiration and awe. It is even difficult to imagine that a writer today may in his own way, from the depths of his soul, extol "love" in literature, and express the view that love ennobles and elevates man, since at present, with our customs becoming so crude, the literature which depicts the cleansing, elevating nature of love must have a special significance. One is even hard put to believe that one among us can write such words, though they may not really represent anything new. But unfortunately, it is only one writer. Today only he, Gorky, is able to write so, and no one else, in all the Soviet Union. And one is terrified to think that after Gorky's death, that one voice too, that single human voice rising from the reality of our life, will be gone too, and all our publishing will become stereotyped, ideological, and tasteless.

March 23

There is no greater pleasure for me than to lie down in my room, dismiss all other thoughts from my mind, and read any classical writer. I like to read Pushkin most. When I am sad and depressed and want to reward myself with the greatest joy, I shut the doors of my house, lie down and begin to read Pushkin, whichever of his works it may be.

Ah, it is still possible to exist in this world, if you have the means that will permit you to do "nothing" for an entire day; that is, dismiss mundane concerns, and stretch out on a cot and read some writer, far removed from our time, and imagine yourself free and independent.

The writer's profession I have chosen is precious for me because it allows me the freedom to do "nothing"; that is, to relax and read. Are there many who can do that? As pleased as I am with this circumstance, I am fully aware that "that pure pleasure" is available to me not nearly as much as I would like. If I should over-indulge it, I will soon be so "pure," both in finances and experiences, that no one will pay me a cent, either for "pure pleasure," or simply for living in the most impure way.

Let our "Marxist" critics say what they wish, the writer "amasses" his "treasure" not consciously, but "subconsciously."

In that is the secret of creating.

---

[1] It was Charents' intention to publish Derian's work. Volume I, which he had edited, was ready in 1937, but never published. For note on Khanjian, see page 135.

[2] The last line of Charents' poem dedicated to Derian, written in 1920 and beginning with the line: "You have already gone away, you no longer exist in this world."

[3] Reference is to the poet and novelist Mekertich Armen (1906-1972).

[4] Armen went to Erevan in the fall of 1925, and not 1926.

[5] Reference is to the poet and novelist Kourken Mahari (1903-1969).

[6] Charents came to know Miasnikian in December 1922 in Moscow.

[7] Derian had gone to Tiflis from St. Petersburg in December 1916, where he remained, with some interruptions, until mid-January of 1917. Then he went to Soukhoumi for a time to convalesce from tuberculosis. Thus Charents could not have seen him then. ("The Rainbow" is dated 1916, Kars—February 1917, Moscow). When he left Soukhoumi, Derian went to Kantsa, his birthplace, via Tiflis (April-May 1917). It is then that Charents probably saw him.

[8] The teahouse, "A Cup of Tea," was established in 1915 on the initiative of Armenian intellectuals, most of them women, for the purpose of aiding refugees and orphans.

[9] A line from Derian's poem, "Carousel," the first two pronouns transposed by Charents.

Declaration of the Three[1]

Armenian poetry is tubercular, and inescapably doomed to die.

Its only justification for existence is the imminence of its death.

Its traditions resemble tubercular children who are unable to bring forth anything but the infection itself.

"Fatherland," "Unblemished Love," "Desert and Loneliness," "Delicate Dusks," "Oblivion and Dreams"[2]—these are the viruses of our literary disease, the symptoms of which are nationalism, romanticism, pessimism, and symbolism.

We venture to make this public diagnosis.

We bring with us fresh air and robust health.

We oppose bourgeois nationalism with proletarian internationalism.

Against "unblemished love," we pit healthy sexual instinct.

For us the "deserts" have become boisterous cities.

In our veins we feel the emotions of the multitudes.

"Delicate Dusks" have been superseded by the red dawn, and the martial trumpet of the struggling class has aroused us from our "forgetful reveries."

We are inspired by the tempo of the masses, and our creativity is directed toward them.

This is what we expect.

1. To liberate poetry from its cloistered rooms, bring it into the streets and to the masses, out of the books and into the living language.

2. To articulate what is contemporary—movement, class struggle, strength, and zeal.

To achieve this, our poetry must have:

a. Rhythm as movement.

b. Image as the focus of the way we live.

c. Style and language as the expression of a given subject and temperament.

Our credo:

May we be rid of the aristocratic opportunists, the cloistered writers, the books slumbering in the libraries, and the women of the salons.

May the living artistic word sustain the creative multitudes.

May the creative masses prevail with their mighty rhythms.

May the proletarian revolution flourish.

[1] This "Declaration" appeared in *Soviet Armenia* on June 14, 1922, signed

by E. Charents, K. Apov, and Azad Veshdooni. According to Apov, it was
written by him and Charents in Veshdooni's home in Tiflis. The "Declara-
tion" was harshly condemned for its negation of the country's literary
heritage and, on the other hand, praised for its determination to recast the
literature in the spirit of the times.

2 The quotes are from Vahan Derian against whom the "Declaration" was
chiefly directed. Charents considered Derian's poetry as the dominant school.

The Deceased Gentleman

Sunday morning I decided to visit one of the museums
in Rome, though I had long since grown weary of every kind
of antiquity. In Rome, as in all Italy, there seem to be two
things that not only bore a person, but also repel him: The
first is macaroni; the second, the antiquities. But I had nothing
to do, I was already suffocating with boredom, and I went.

Obviously I anticipated nothing unusual in the visit. But—
can you conceive of it?—I came very close to being wrong.
I say "close" because the unexpected thing I fortuitously came
across in that museum did not seem to really belong there . . .
though of course I can't be sure of that; I leave it to the reader
to resolve that "delicate" question himself, in whatever way
he can.

I repeat that I entered the halls of the museum without
the slightest expectation of any surprise and, still very much
indifferent, began to look, first at the statues and then at the
paintings. I had just entered the paintings gallery. I was alone
in the hall. Not a single person besides myself. It was early
morning and the estimable tourists, those—as I would describe
them—international parasites who are so enamored of every
kind of antiquity had not yet been mobilized. I was looking
at some famous painting of some famous painter. I can recall

neither the name of the master nor that of the painting. I remember only that the painting showed an emaciated, wooden, moribund face, and as it is generally said, on the "forehead there was suffering and at the same time the mark of the other world." It was an early Renaissance Christ, and obviously not a finished painting, but a sketch or a study. I was just getting ready, as they say, to "delve" into that wonder of early Renaissance art when someone, approaching me from behind, grasped my arm in a familiar manner. I was momentarily bewildered. I had literally no acquaintances in Rome but that in itself would not have mattered; the suddenness of the contact was enough to catch me off guard. But there was another more curious circumstance which left the sort of impression on me I couldn't quite make out. When, responding to the uncertain contact of his fingers, I turned to look at the man who had approached me so unexpectedly, an almost mystical sensation swept over me from the first moment. I think I even recoiled involuntarily; my eyes may have been blurred; I don't know; I don't remember how it all happened; but one thing I remember clearly, as brightly as the light of the sun. It was the eyes of that person, at first glance unknown to me, eyes that were so much like the grieving, smiling eyes of the Christ in that famous painting on the wall. This is what confused me at first and even, as I have suggested, turned my thoughts to the supernatural. For a brief moment I felt that he was himself the very Christ of the early Renaissance who by some eerie spell of nature had descended from the painting and was staring at me, the devil knows with what intentions. The thought occurred to me that, should I venture to turn around for another look at the wall, I would no longer see anything there, except for the gilded frame of the painting. And perhaps that was the case, I don't know. (So many odd things happen in this strange world of ours. I thought suddenly of one of Upton Sinclair's novels, and of Edgar Allan Poe.) But for one reason or another, I was unable to verify that suspicion. Just as I was about to turn my head toward the painting, the stranger spoke.

"Ah, if I am not mistaken, you must be Mr. Charents," he exclaimed in a voice that was both human and natural. And, summoned suddenly back to reality, I had the vague recollection of having met this man before. At that point another peculiar element contributed to my confusion, but in a different way. It was my recollection now that this man was one I had seen years ago in a coffin. My feeling was simply that, by some mysterious heavenly miracle, I was facing a living corpse; perhaps not a living corpse exactly. It might be more accurate to say, a corpse now resurrected, whom I had seen with my own eyes in the coffin, whom I had accompanied to the cemetery, and on whom I had myself thrown a handful of earth, as is the custom, "for the peace of his soul." And here, suddenly, and in such an amazing manner, that dead man materialized before me, as though shooting out of the ground or the wall, and grasped my arm, asking with serene composure whether I was not perhaps so and so, even addressing me, as you may have noticed, as "Mister," an appropriate form during his lifetime. You will agree that my feelings were far from common, particularly since, even as a child, I stubbornly resisted any idea of the existence of another world, despite my mother's persistent entreaties. But however different my inclinations may have been, proof remains proof, and the evidence was that this man, by whatever path he had arrived here, was standing at my side, looking amiably into my eyes, and pressing my hand with the warmth of friendship.

What was there for me to do, please tell me, if not to prevent giving him the impression that I was afraid of him, and with equal calmness shake his hand and even fashion on my face a sweet smile of cordiality? And that is just what I did, especially since at that very moment I recalled everything about the Deceased Gentleman (permit me to refer to him as such because I am hard put to give him a more suitable name); I recalled that while he was still alive, before he resettled in the other world, he was an editor of a leading party's principal newspaper,[1] for which he wrote very militant editorials about the day's significant issues. I also remembered that, besides being an editor, he was a party "figure," a prominent personality, virtually a pillar of that party, that he was known for his considerable scientific knowledge and theoretical understanding. I also remembered his death[2] which occurred in unusual circumstances. It may even be said that, together with many of his friends, he died quite suddenly. Was it sunstroke, perhaps, or a nervous breakdown? I don't know. I remembered only that his was an unusual death; the particulars were forgotten. Besides these, I also recalled that in Erevan some priests, deacons, and others who have some relation to religion were saying that the Deceased Gentleman was also publishing a journal in that other world, by the name of "Celestial and Divine Hope," in which, according to his old custom, he was writing occasional articles and editorials, now concerned with some vital questions, such as the resurrection of the dead, the immortality of the soul, the terrifying last judgment, and so on. In a word, these recollections sufficiently reassured me, enabling me in my turn, as I said, to grip his hand, and answer politely:

"It has come back to me. I remember now. You, I think, are so and so who used to edit a paper from time to time . . ."

"That's the one, exactly," the Deceased Gentleman hurried to confirm. "But you, do you realize you have changed quite a bit, Mr. Charents? You have lost some weight, and have become perhaps a little more serious. What I mean is that you have grown, matured. I had no other thought in mind."

"Well, I understand, sir, of course. It could not have been otherwise. Considerable time has passed, and you too have changed. You have aged, become thinner, I think, or is it that you're paler or a trifle jaundiced?"

"That's precisely the case." Once again the Deceased Gentleman was quick to answer. "You were still an adolescent at the time, perhaps a little beyond adolescence, 22 or 23 years old."

"Yes, 22 or 23." My echo had an ethereal tone, rising from the misty nostalgia of those years. But the Deceased Gentleman went on, effectively dispersing my melancholy.

"I am very pleased to see you, I can't say how happy. Do you know what I would like?" He looked at me fondly and squeezed my arm again, as if I were a dear cousin. "I want some information about our beloved country, just a few things . . ."

"With pleasure. I am completely at your disposal," I hastened to assure the Deceased Gentleman, although, I could not hide it, I was rather astonished that the dead could be interested in the living. But I was relieved by the recollection of my mother's belief that the dead never forget the living, always seek them out in fact. They emerge from the cemeteries at night and for long intervals, till daybreak, wander through neighboring cities and villages, entering all the houses in turn, and with a bitter supernatural yearning roam among the places where they once lived and visited. Remembering my mother's beliefs, authoritative in such areas, I was prepared to give the Deceased Gentleman detailed and accurate information about anything he wished to know, not so much out of respect for him, for that Deceased Gentleman, as for my mother's precious memory, and especially her injunction that we must not alienate or recoil from the dead, but should in fact show compassion toward them. This last recollection touched me so deeply that my eyes filled with tears as I gazed at the Deceased Gentleman; it was only then that I seemed to notice the unusual characteristics of his face. It suddenly struck me that the yellowish-blue skin drawn tautly over his face, seemed no more than an illusion. I felt sure that if I continued to look at it for a minute or two, it would suddenly melt away and vanish; and only a skull would be left, with yellow teeth, a broken nose, and large empty holes instead of eyes. But at that instant, the Deceased Gentleman began to talk again, and

I did not have an opportunity to examine that momentary sensation any further.

"Yes, Mr. Charents, just a few bits of news," the Deceased Gentleman began. "Oh, if you only knew how much I love Erevan. Can you believe that I am even thinking of going there again? Going . . . whatever the consequences. Let come what may. But spectacular means are needed, and I don't have such means. If I did, I most certainly would go, but secretly of course. Legally, I would not be allowed." (I don't know why, but I mused in Russian: Still the same. And who is there that would permit the dead to walk about freely, in broad daylight, on Abovian Street? I can imagine how my mother would have reacted to such an event, if she were still alive.) "Can you imagine such a thing?" the Deceased Gentleman continued. "Let me tell you about an interesting incident . . . I always say to my wife that no matter what happens, I have to go to Erevan. On her part, she insists that I must not go. But I keep saying that I will, even if they were to shoot me.

"Though I express myself in this manner, I am convinced they would not shoot me; the most they would do is to put me in jail. Ah, Mr. Charents, have we spent so little time in jail? We have squatted in czarist prisons, and we'll squat in bolshevik ones too. What's the difference? There was the time when, after a heated discussion, I fell asleep and, as you can imagine, had a strange dream. I dreamt I had gone to Erevan; and that they had arrested me, and turned me over to the Cheka . . . 10- and 12-year old Chekists had gathered around me—children, boys and girls—with swords and hatchets, eager to attack me, kill me, tear me apart. They stuck their tongues out, made ugly faces, shoved, laughed, and swore; in a word, the same old story. I woke up drenched in sweat; and related the dream to my wife . . . 'Didn't I tell you?' she shouted angrily."

The Deceased Gentleman took a breath at this point, and was silent. As you may have noted, he finished his last sentence in such a way as to imply that more was to come. But it turned out that he had already said what he had intended to say. Now he was looking at me triumphantly, a sly smile on his face, apparently waiting for a response.

"Listen to your wife," I told him in all seriousness.

"But I cannot be without Erevan," he said plaintively. "Whatever happens, I must go . . . do you hear?"

"I hear," I replied calmly. He continued.

"Oh, you cannot understand what a fatherland means; and what yearning for a fatherland can be . . . though, forgive me, you may perhaps personally understand . . . there is evidence of this in your "I Love the Sun-baked Taste of Armenian Words." Oh I admire that poem of yours; I have even reprinted it in my paper. Do you know the two things I can never forget? One is the sunrise on the plain of Ararat; and the other, strange memory . . . Have you been in Etchmiadzin?"

"Yes."

"Then you are familiar with the Kevorkian Seminary. I was a lecturer there.[3] In the evenings, the students used to gather in the dining hall and after supper they used to sing, 'Our Fatherland,' I mean 'Our Father, who art . . .' [I am not exaggerating or "embellishing" this; the Deceased Gentleman actually confused the patriotic song with the Lord's Prayer. But he quickly corrected himself. It should be noted that the Deceased Gentleman's words are being set down here almost verbatim.] Yes, they sang the Lord's Prayer. It was very beautiful. I have not forgotten it. The feeling might seem ridiculous to you, even 'counter-revolutionary,' but . . ."

He fell silent again. In general, as already noted, he liked to talk in half-finished sentences. It seemed to be a kind of style with which he was trying to keep me dangling in the uncertainty of uncompleted thoughts.

"But what?" I asked, looking directly into his eyes.

"What else?" he smiled and continued. "The fatherland is a sweet thing, Mr. Charents, and nothing can take its place . . . I remember the last time they were taking me away . . ."

(I thought he was about to say "cemetery," but instead he said . . .)

". . . from Erevan. We were in a closed car. They had searched us and stripped us of our possessions. But I had managed to conceal my small pen, which I have kept to this day as a sacred object; here it is." He took a small, blackened pen from his vest pocket, returning it almost immediately. "I pierced the curtain of the car with the penpoint, and was able to look out. I wanted to see Erevan for the last time, at whatever price, but it was dark outside, raining, and nothing was visible, except for the wall opposite us. But—just imagine—at that moment, that wall was everything to me, more precious than anything . . ."

He was quiet again, looking not at me, but to one side, as though ashamed of the candor of his deeply emotional expression.

"I understand," I said gently, touched by his embarrassment. "But what prevents your return to Erevan, especially since your patriotic longing is so urgent?"

I confess that there was not much logic in my words, but moved as I was by the Deceased Gentleman's hesitancy, I seemed to forget for a moment my own mother's advice, as well as the warnings of his own wife, with which, just a little earlier, I had agreed. But as it turned out, the Deceased Gentleman was waiting for just that.

"What!" He was stunned. "What prevents me from returning? You are preventing it, Mr. Charents, your government is preventing it. Tell me how, I beg of you, I can set foot into Erevan as long as your government still exists, and as long as I have not renounced my sacred vow never to live under two kinds of authority, one Turkish, the other bolshevik."

"But under what system have you consented to live now?" I asked, I don't know why, and, recalling the manner in which the Gentleman became Deceased, added: "No doubt some supreme celestial authority . . ."

"No," he shouted, "Egyptian!"

"English, that is," I interjected, remembering the Deceased's other world. The Gentleman was furious.

"Oh, no, you are mistaken, Mr. Charents. Egyptian, not English. This is where you make your biggest mistake. It is obvious that you haven't been to Egypt, otherwise you wouldn't, forgive my bluntness, say such a childish thing which, in all likelihood, you have learned from your pamphlets and newspapers. And that is the most astonishing thing of all, how a handful of people, a mere fifty million, can rule three-quarters of the universe. [I remember clearly that the Deceased Gentleman said "the universe" and not the world.] To understand this astounding phenomenon it is imperative at the very least not to be . . . a bolshevik! Yes, my dear sir, it is precisely on this point that you make your most serious error. It is this that you cannot and will never be able to see. And it is this that represents the chief difference between the oppressive bolshevik tyranny and enlightened English imperialism . . ."

This is exactly what the Deceased Gentleman said: "Enlightened imperialism." I thought he was joking but soon saw that he was completely serious. Even his eyes sparkled with a "sacred fervor"; it was with that kind of fervor that he continued.

"Let me explain it for you to see. You go to Egypt, live there for one, two, five, ten years, and—just imagine—you do not see any Englishmen, nor hear the English language, nor come across English dress. In government offices, all are Arabs who speak Arabic, dress in Arabic clothing, and follow Arabic customs. If you have any business to transact, you must of course first go through at least six rooms of a given establishment where all sorts of Arab functionaries will meet with you; it is only in the seventh and last room that you will meet with an English rascal on whom the final decision of your business depends . . ."

I was astonished that he had actually said "rascal," but the Deceased Gentleman went on.

"Note also that you will find that English rascal with his legs folded under him and a fez on his head; and he will talk to you not in English, but in Arabic; and only from his blond hair and blue eyes will you be able to determine that you are dealing with an Englishman and not a real Arab."

"It is cunningly contrived, and we have known all about that for a long time . . ." I began to object, but he stopped me there.

"Yes, if you wish to consider it no more than cunning, consider as something negative the national customs, the mother tongue, the native habits, the things which are the essential elements of every national civilization, and not of international lawlessness . . . yes, and so it is for all of enlightened mankind, which does not of course include your Third International, which should more appropriately be called the Russian National . . ."

I made an impatient gesture, indicating disagreement, but I looked at the Deceased Gentleman's face and saw that it would be futile to argue.

I was amazed to find that the dead are capable of so much enthusiasm, something which had apparently escaped my dear mother's attention.

In any event I considered it prudent to remain silent, and allow the Deceased Gentleman to continue.

"Yes, the Russian National. Are you perhaps aware that from Ivan Kalita[4] to Lenin and Chernov,[5] who will arrive tomorrow . . ."

"Chernov?"

"Yes, yes, to Chernov, who will come tomorrow; all those Russian rulers have been occupied and will continue to be occupied with nothing else but expanding Russian territory."

"Old wives' tales . . ."

I thought my contemptuous remark might enrage the Deceased Gentleman; but to my amazement as soon as he heard it he abruptly terminated his monologue, and looked at me with such compassionate, though disapproving eyes that

I was again reminded of my mother's views on the misery and aggressiveness of the dead. And, as I looked at him, the impression grew that the yellowish-blue skin stretched over his face was a mask of some sort. The Deceased Gentleman, however, resumed with some bitterness.

"Of course, Mr. Charents, you are convinced that if it were proposed to the Arabs of Egypt to accept the Russian 'Red International's' 'dictatorship of the peasants and workers,' instead of the 'bloodthirsty imperialism' of the English, all the Arabs would leap at the opportunity, with the Arab 'peasants and workers' leading the parade—all these in quotes of course. But you are mistaken, Mr. Charents, bitterly mistaken. And this mistake, for you personally, derives from an inability to conceive of what a blessing the enlightened English imperialism is for the Arab peasantry."

"I don't think," I said, unable to restrain myself any longer "that 'enlightened imperialism' is a greater blessing for the Egyptian peasant than the latter is for the 'enlightened imperialism.' And please tell me, sir, why, if you have so high a regard for enlightened English imperialism, you resent it when you are called agents of that imperialism?"

I had barely finished when suddenly something altogether unexpected occurred, the shock of the surprise itself stirring a strange fear in me. As I said, I had barely finished my sentence when suddenly the Deceased Gentleman grabbed my arm and—just imagine it—laughed out loud, exactly as a living person would have laughed. I could anticipate anything from the Deceased Gentleman, except laughter. It is terrifying when the dead laugh at the living . . . disquieting. My dismay would surely have deepened but for the Deceased Gentleman's interjection.

"Ha, ha, ha! Who said we are resentful? And why doesn't it bother you that you are an agent of a bloodthirsty bolshevik tyranny? And without even being aware of it!"

He roared with laughter once again. He stopped and was about to say something, but hesitated and suddenly changed the direction of the conversation.

"Please tell me about construction work in Armenia. It interests me very much. What streets have been repaired in Erevan?"

I told him what he wanted to know in detail, adding that I was puzzled by the narrow scope of the question. Do the streets of Erevan represent the most critical aspect of construction in Armenia? Why doesn't the Gentleman ask about the Shirak Canal, Erevan's hydroelectric station, Leninakan's textile factory, the mines of Allaverdi and Ghapan, and things of this order, which should generate a bit more interest in any "patriot" than the streets of Erevan? But this did not succeed in distracting the Deceased Gentleman.

"Do you know what?" he asked quite seriously. "I don't believe in the creative work of Soviet Armenia."

"What is the basis of your disbelief?"

"The reports we receive. You are generally mistaken to think we have no contacts in the country. And the idea of yours that Dashnagtsoutioun is dead there is childish. Dashnagtsoutioun survives; for the present, however, without any plans to fight.

"The time shall come when it will re-emerge. Once the Russian forces leave Armenia, the peasants and workers of the country, the entire population without exception, and as one person, will rally to Dashnagtsoutioun. You do not comprehend the powerful lure of Dashnagtsoutioun. It is the kind of force that binds all Armenians together, yes, all Armenians, without exception."

"Especially the priests and the kulaks."

"Yes, the priests and the kulaks too. And that is something one cannot be a bolshevik and understand. Cast aside your idiotic class theory, Mr. Charents, and particularly your socialism. There is no socialism or anything like it for Dashnagtsoutioun. This is a compact mass which no force can tear asunder. The only reason for the collapse of its government is that the party has always been devoid of the desire to rule."

"Disregarding the fact," I said almost automatically, "that to cling to that apparently undesired rule even a brief moment longer, it did not hesitate to sacrifice Kars, Sarighamish, and Alexandropol . . ."

I anticipated an angry emotional reaction; but his response was sober.

"Any party would have conducted itself in the same way, any party at the head of a government. If it had been you, you would not have left earlier either. And if we left in 1920, it was only because Dashnagtsoutioun lacked the lust for power."

"There was scarcely anything else left to do when, as they say, 'the knife had reached the bone,' that is, the bolshevik knife."

Once again, as he had done earlier, the Deceased Gentleman laughed loudly, but immediately became serious when he added:

"It is perhaps unknown to you that we voluntarily surrendered the government for the purpose of saving the people. And we did save the people by withdrawing from the government."

"Then you agree that the survival of the people depended in the first instance on your being forced out of the government."

"What do you mean 'forced'; we left of our own accord," the Deceased Gentleman protested. After a brief silence, he changed the subject once again.

"Eh, let's dispense with this kind of talk, Mr. Charents. Tell me about construction in Armenia."

"But didn't you say that you didn't believe in our creative abilities? What's the point then . . ?"

And it was here that our conversation reached a dramatic culmination, the Deceased Gentleman articulating his most relevant opinion, the most ingenious expression of a moribund philosophy, through which he revealed the real character of his sacred "patriotic feelings."

"Do you know what?" he said. "It is our conviction that whatever you are building in the country today, you are building for us. So our feeling is, the more the better."

"Are you so convinced of that?"

"Yes, without a single doubt."

"And when do you plan on returning to take over all those treasures, so hateful to you, of bolshevik initiative?"

"In two years; yes, two years."

"Perhaps even sooner, don't you think? Why so late? Can you last till then? You look as though you are starving. Perhaps we should go to a cafe."

"Are there cafes in Armenia?" the Deceased Gentleman inquired, making a strange though perhaps not unexpected digression. He looked at me inquisitively. Again, and for the last time, I remembered my mother's convictions about the dead having extraordinary appetites; to satisfy themselves, they turned into hyenas and attacked children at night. I answered.

"No, there aren't any. There are no cafes in Armenia. There are no restaurants either. There the people eat and sleep in the streets, on sidewalks. The meetings of the Soviet council are held on the beautiful banks of the Zankou, for lack of an appropriate place. Do you know, incidentally, that one of your colleagues asked me once whether the women in Soviet Armenia use white under garments. Perhaps the question too interests you? I can provide you with the most precise and accurate reply. The women in Soviet Armenia have no white underwear. They don't use any. They haven't developed the habit of using any. They walk around naked on Abovian Street, like Adam and Eve in Paradise. Are you satisfied? Goodbye!"

"Are you annoyed, Mr. Charents?" the Deceased Gentleman was surprisingly gentle. "Please, don't be. Before parting I would like to ask you to do a small favor for me in Erevan."

He took out a letter from his pocket and handed it to me.

"Please give this to my mother, when you return to Erevan

. . . Ah, how I envy you, that you will be there soon. But I won't despair. Two years from now . . ."

"Blessed are the faithful, for theirs is the Kingdom of Heaven," I said, accepting the letter and shaking his hand. A moment later, after I had slipped the letter into my breast pocket, the Deceased Gentleman had vanished.

I looked around, as if aroused from a dream. I was sitting on the marble steps, near the entrance of one of Rome's renowned museums. It appears that we had moved in that direction as we talked, and sat together on those steps.

The Deceased Gentleman was not there. I reached into my pocket and took out the letter; I read the address. If it had not been for that letter, it would have been difficult to believe that all this had happened. I remembered his last words and murmured to myself, and at the same time to the beloved specter of my mother:

"The dead must miss those who remain alive; and the dead desire to eat. They have astonishing appetites. And, dear mother, it is not surprising that they turn into hyenas and attack children at night. Your mistake, mother, was that you feared them. I assure you that there is no need to be afraid. If you don't believe this, ask your Komsomols."[6]

And I walked, feeling some elation, toward the cafe to have a glass of beer.

Rome, February 16, 1925

The character of the "Deceased Gentleman" derives from the noted Dashnagtsagan leader, Vahan Navasardian (1886-1956), who in his turn described his meeting with Charents in his book, *Charents* (Memoirs and Meditations), Cairo, 1957. He also mentions the letter he asked Charents to deliver to his mother. Navasardian's mother was furious when she read this piece by Charents, and went to the editorial office of "Soviet Armenia" to confront the poet. But Charents had not yet returned to Armenia. Several months later a young man knocked at her door, introduced himself as Charents and, in her words, "spoke so sweetly, so nicely and gently that I completely forgot my anger, and I invited him to come the following Sunday for Gharabagh Keofteh"—a famous dish of the region from which the Navasardians had come.

[1] Beginning on July 16, 1918, Navasardian edited the daily "Horizon," the Dashnagtsagan party organ in Tiflis. In 1922 he began editing the same party's daily, "Hoosaper," in Cairo, Egypt.

[2] Reference is to the fall in 1920 of the Armenian Republic, which was ruled by the Dashnagtsagan party.

[3] In 1916-1917 Navasardian taught the Russian language and history at the Kevorkian Seminary in Etchmiadzin.

[4] Ivan Kalita, the Prince of Moscow, Ivan I, who ruled between 1325 and 1340.

[5] M.V. Chernov (1876-1952) was a Russian political figure, later a White Russian emigre.

[6] Communist Youth Organization.

Letters

Controversy was certain to pursue a writer of Charents' caliber. At times he even appeared to seek it, virtually encouraging it by the new directions his work explored. He was attacked during his lifetime for sins which in other circumstances would be deemed virtues, as they were by his own people a couple of decades later. It is hardly possible to draw accurate impressions about Charents and his work from these since they were often personally or politically motivated. Charents was sometimes subjected to similar treatment even in the diaspora.

The fiftieth anniversary of Charents' death will be marked in November 1987. By then the personal denigrations may have finally settled into the historical record of a confused time, and attention will center on the poet's work and achievement. It is from the writing itself that the man and artist will be judged. And in this regard, his letters constitute a significant source, revealing the person behind the work perhaps more than the poetry, fiction and memoirs.

We have included a significant number of his published letters, omitting no more than a handful of those available. Even a casual reading reveals the pressing financial need Charents had to contend with. His repeated requests for money may seem to mark him as excessively materialistic; in the end it is no more than an anxiety for practical recognition and for the security of himself and his family. The concern is articulated movingly in his statement to the secretariat of the Armenian Writers' Union in 1935, two years before his death.

He had apparently come full circle; he had begun with limited means and towards the end was still worried about "securing a minimum livelihood for myself and my family."

Strangely, there are very few letters between 1925 and 1933. Did he suddenly stop writing? Not likely. An explanation can be found in the numerous memoirs of Charents' contemporaries—who, in chronicling their contacts with the poet, mention having received many letters, expressing regret at having lost them. One cannot escape a nagging thought about this explanation. Is it reasonable to suppose that so many letters from a particular period could all be lost? Or is it more logical to suspect that they were destroyed in an effort to eradicate any evidence of association with the pre-eminent figure of Armenian letters who had become a non-person?

What letters remain are sufficient to provide an adequate measure of the man and artist. They offer a sense of his judgment of various literary figures and events in Russia and in Armenia. He is fair in his evaluation of Armenian writers, and careful not to let extraneous considerations interfere with his literary appraisal. Some of the letters surely eluded the censor's attention, encouraging greater latitude in his expression. But his poetry, published and unpublished, also underlines his predominant concern for artistic values.

Whatever else one might conclude from these letters, one thing seems to be clear: Charents emerges as a warm, considerate and courageous individual, an impression corroborated by his poetry, as well as by the memoirs of those who had come to know him well. The rest, paraphrasing the poet himself, is in his work.

Arshavir Khondgarian (1889-1957): A poet and translator.

Comrade Khondgarian,

I received your letter and, as I said in my telegram, I agree that the honorarium be paid in cash, by installments, as you suggested. Although you made no mention of it in your letter, I think it is fair to assume that payment will be in Tiflis currency (either Georgian[1] or Pon[2], it's all the same). You noted that the price of my book will be set at 30 rubles, so that is what it will be worth in either Pon or Georgian currency. By that calculation you had reckoned that 320 copies will bring 9,600 rubles; and you expect to pay ten to twelve. I think it should be 12,000. And as to the installments, I think I should receive 5,000 rubles on publication of the book, and the rest later, whenever feasible. I really don't think that business should figure more importantly in our relationship than friendship. I suppose that by the time you receive this letter, publication of the book will have started. Please send me about 20 copies, as soon as they are available, for close friends and associates; as for the 5,000 rubles, forward it to Mr. Karekin Levonian as quickly as possible. If I seem anxious about this, it is because I bought a supply of paper in Tiflis at a very good price, and the sooner I pay for it, the better it will be for me. If you think it is necessary (you have my complete confidence), you can send me the company's[3] official contract for the publication of my book.

If for any reason you find it inappropriate to pay in cash, I will agree to accept payment in books, but only on condition that the price is not printed in the copies given to me. (The covers for these copies can be printed separately with the price deleted. Nothing more.)

Please turn over all unused manuscripts to the same Mr. Karekin Levonian.

I would like to make some suggestions about the design of the book. As I told you earlier, the lines should not begin with upper case letters, which are to be used only after periods.

It would be nice, if it is possible, to have the last two or three pages blank. I would also prefer to have no illustrations at all, no floral or other designs included in the text. The spelling and punctuation must remain as given.

I have revised the poem "You are bronze, you are fire," and since I do not remember whether the text you have is the earlier or revised version, I enclose a copy of the poem as it should appear. Please compare it with the copy you have.

Nothing more. Please accept my friendly greetings.

Yours,

Eghishe Charents

Erevan, April 22, 1920

My address is the same.[4] Please write to me quickly.

[1] The currency used by the Mensheviks.
[2] The currency used by the Transcaucasian Commissariat.
[3] Probably the Armenian publishing house (perhaps the only one) in Tiflis, M. Eprikian & Co., 1919-1920.
[4] In 1920, according to K. Apov, Charents used Terenig Temirjian's office in Erevan. By 1921 it had become Charents' office.

Karekin Levonian (1872-1947): Editor of "Kegharvest"; he reviewed Charents' "Danteesque Legend" in 1916. Beginning in 1917, Charents sent him poems for publication in "Kegharvest."

The esteemed Karekin Levonian,

For the next issue of "Kegharvest," I had sent you five poems titled, "Your Profile in Stained Glass."[1] Please do not consider them for publication; I'll send you new material I have two notebooks of poems with Arshavir Khondgarian. I have written asking him to give those notebooks to you, in the hope that you may forward them to me. Please, Mr. Levonian, keep those books with you until such time as I can manage to get them. I have no other acquaintances there, and am extremely sorry for bothering you with such burdensome requests.

If Arshavir Khondgarian brings you the notebooks, please do not publish anything from them. Should any friends be traveling this way, send what materials of mine you may have along with them. Otherwise, hold on to them until I can make arrangements to get them.

Accept my deepest respects.

Yours,
Eghishe Charents

Erevan, September 1920

Again, please forgive me for bothering you.

[1] In Armenia, a vari-colored glass which is melted and used to cover metal surfaces as adornment.

Dear Karekin Levonian:

I had sent you five poems titled "Your Profile in Stained Glass" for "Kegharvest." I later wrote you about them, but I don't know whether that letter will reach you or not. I beg you not to publish this work, or any of the other material of mine which you may have. I'll send you new material; exactly when, I do not know. As to the manuscripts you have, please return them to me with some suitable person.

Accept my deepest respects.

Yours,
Eghishe Charents

Erevan, September 20, 1920

Laylee (Parantsem Sahakian-Der Mekertichian, 1884-1951): A poet Charents met in September 1920, in Erevan.

Laylee Dear,

I write this letter to you as to an old friend, since I don't

have anyone close here (or anywhere); and I cannot under-
stand how you became so close to me in so short a time. Lately,
I have become sad, very sad, with a sense of being mean-
ingless. Writing, even living, seems to be pointless. At no other
time have I ever been so bored with the world. That's how
it is, dear Laylee. And with wine and cognac hard to get, it's
even worse, almost unbearable. Then there is the work. I have
been assigned the section on art[1] by the Commissariat of
Culture. Art is fine, but free time and pleasure are better for
a lonely man. Only last year I wrote a small poem about that
wretched loneliness.

> *The lights that are to come are red and dark*
> *Red, made of fire, but ah, they cannot soothe.*
>
> *And who oall on them*
> *Are alone, are sad, are helpless and sad.*
>
> *A familiar grief whines in my heart*
> *The lights are far off, without care, without woe.*

It is plain to me that only devastation can move me, the
collapse of the mobs; what they call "constructive work" does
not interest me all that much. I have one wish now, to go to
the land of fire, or to the ocean, to get a sense of the sea and
the sand, or as the brilliant Derian says:

> *And with my prodigal brother, under a wall*
> *I wanted to die wretched and unremembered.*[2]

It is better that way, Laylee. You are good too. And the
world. Everything is good, and best of all is to die
unremembered, dear, or in the popular phrase, "die a dog's
death."
It is a pointless letter I'm writing, Laylee dear; I feel lost.
I have lost my mind, my head. If at least they had sent me
to Moscow,[3] if they had said, Charents, go on to Moscow, there

we will give you a glass of water and a slice of bread; live there till you die. My letter seems to be turning into an interminable plaint. Don't worry about it; this may be good too, Laylee.

You know, Laylee, you would do well to come here, come and take over the section on art. It is meant for you, a job you can do well. I too will benefit; I can go to Moscow. I must say, Laylee, that I did not receive your last letter; it must have been lost; it pained my heart not to have received it. Write again, I want so much to hear a word from you, because a word from you will save me. You can exert a strong will and influence on me; sometimes I feel afraid of you. That is good too, Laylee, to be in awe of an influence one cherishes. I am enclosing three ballads with this letter. These are the last I have written, and not a line since, and I don't know if I will be able to write another.

Accept my most sincere respects and greetings.

Yours,

Eghishe Charents

Erevan, January 10, 1921

---

[1] Charents was placed in charge of art at the Commissariat of Culture in 1920.

[2] These are the last two lines of a Derian poem which begins with, "I love those who are mad and homeless." The poem first appeared in *The Cooperative of Armenia,* July 15, 1920, in which two Charents poems, "To the Memory of Vahan Derian," also appeared.

[3] Charents went to Moscow to study in July 1921.

Dear Laylee,

My warmest regards and greetings.

My courier is my wife. I have been married.[1] She is a nice girl. I ask that you accept and love her.

What have you been doing? I was told that you have been intending to write to me, but you have not written. I wonder why. Why forget a friend so soon? You know that I respect and am fond of you. I respect you a great deal. I always think of you and despair that I do not hear from you. And you? What can one do? But then, women can't be blamed, I suppose; women always forget quickly. It is written on their foreheads. You cannot change what is written on the forehead.

But it is the sadness of friendship, respect for what is good, luminous, that cannot be driven from the heart.

Laylee, Laylee. Dear Laylee.

I wish you would write to me, I wish it very much. I have composed seven ballads for you, one of them titled "Buffoon."[2] It suits me perfectly; it is I. Nothing goes well. And all that means is that it is a lie. Laylee, Laylee. Dear Laylee.

What are you up to? I am married now; I don't drink anymore. But now that my wife has left, it will be sad. She is a nice girl, Laylee. You might well say, What do I care? Just like that. Write to me. Don't forget.

I kiss your hands,
Charents

Erevan, June 18, 1921

P.S.: I almost forgot. My manuscripts are with Arshavir Khondgarian, two volumes of them. One is *Sacrificial Fire;* the other, *Profile in Stained Glass.* Please take them from him and give them to my wife, or tell him to give them to her directly. Do you remember? You had promised me to write poems. It reminded me of the feathers of Hamsun's Lieutenant.[3] Two feathers. Perhaps it was a girl who sent the feathers to the lieutenant. A distant, unknown girl.

I am not feeling well, my disposition, that is, sentimental. "Do you know that there is a wart under the nose of the Persian Shah?"[4]

I am writing triolets now. Triolets to the sun.[5] Laylee, dear Laylee. I miss you so much. Laylee, Laylee. Dear Laylee.

Charents

[1] Arpenig (Der Asdvadsadrian) Charents (1889-1927), whom Charents mar-

ried in May or June 1921.

² From the volume, *The Street Bitch*.

³ Protagonist of Knut Hamsun's (1859-1952) novel, *Pan*.

⁴ A Russian proverb.

⁵ The sequel to *Octets to the Sun*, written in May-June 1921, in Erevan.

Hovhaness Toumanian (1869-1923): Poet and author of short stories and legends. The high esteem in which he was held is reflected in the affectionate designation of him as "Poet of All Armenians," much like the title of the Supreme Patriarch of the Armenian Church—"Catholicos of All Armenians."

Comrade Toumanian,

I regret very much that I could not visit you before my departure. With this note I have enclosed 12 triolet-like songs. If you deem it appropriate, publish them in the book.¹ Accept my deepest respects and greetings.

Yours,

Eghishe Charents

Tiflis, July 8, 1921

¹ According to accounts of contemporaries (D. Hakhoumian, M. Kevorkian), a volume of poems by Armenian writers was to have been published in Tiflis, edited by Hovhaness Toumanian and titled *New Day*. But the project was not realized.

Dear Laylee,

It is with such longing that I write those words, "Dear Laylee." It might seem that I am writing to the sun, to the world, to all mankind, to everything I love most, and love in the way that childhood is loved.

Laylee, dear Laylee, I miss you very much. I say to myself, there was an old world by the name of Nayiri. That world was mine. It was sun, light, blue and distant. There were fruits, grapes, so much; peaches full like lips, fresh as a girl's cheeks, and peaches that resembled a sick woman; and honey-dew melons, golden-hipped Semiramis. Ah, artists are such stupid creatures, describing the fruit they paint as "nature morte." They are the ones who are dead, not the fruit. I want it to be hot, hot. And the sky blue, Laylee, like steel, or the glint of the sea; and fruit, abundant, ripe, colorful; and let there be Laylee, and her eyes, and a smile that stings (and hot like the sun).

It is such things that I seem to be thinking about, confined to one corner of a dormitory, where twenty people are living. My wife has been sleeping on what is called a "bed." What could she be thinking about, Laylee? She is a fine girl, Laylee. I love her very much, as much as Semiramis loved Ara.[1] And, imagine, Laylee, to be married at twenty-three, be a poet, a lover, and suddenly find oneself in a dormitory, where there is not even a decent place to sleep, half-hungry, half-sick. Then there is the winter to think about; and my wife, Arpig. Dear Laylee.

I am in an impossible situation, Laylee. I came here to enter the university, but here I am in a dormitory, because the state university does not have its own facilities, and does not provide board. As for me, I don't have a single kopeck. I don't know where to turn or what to do. Perhaps for the thousandth time I keep thinking about the darkness of our native faces; they are so black, so dark, so heavy, Laylee. My condition is worse than hopeless. On the one hand, Moscow is inspiring; you want to be educated, to write, conceive great thoughts, magnificent plans; on the other hand, there is the dormitory, and my wife with not enough to eat, and not a single familiar face. I don't want to return to Armenia, but I can't stay here either. What is there to do? Imagine, Laylee, how desperate things must have been that I felt compelled to write a letter . . . and to whom? . . . to Makintsian.[2] The last one in the world I would want to write to. But I wrote because I love my wife, and my wife is starving. Do you know what it means when a man's wife is starving?

They have no right to make us starve, Laylee.

Farewell. My heart is beating rapidly. I have to stop. My lips reach with longing from the darkness of this dormitory all the way to the Caucasus, so that they may kiss Laylee.

Charents

P.S.: I beg you to write. I want so much to hear from you. Laylee, I wanted to write about something that affects and saddens me deeply, modern Russian literature. What was a vast and powerful literature has become small, graceless and petty. On one side we have the insubstantial work of the traditionalists (though there is one gifted man among them, Sergei Esenin); on the other side are the proletarian writers, among whom there is not even a single person of talent. And what hurts the most is that I cannot even attend their meetings because the admission fee is 1,000 rubles. I went once.[3] I wondered if these people realized that if I were among them, they would have had a real proletarian poet. When one does not have anything else, it cannot do any harm to have boundless self-esteem.

Greetings once again, and again I wait for your letters. And greetings from my wife.

Yours,
Charents

Moscow, August 21, 1921

---

[1] Reference is to the Armenian legend, "Ara the Beautiful and Semiramis." One of the poems in *The Street Bitch* is titled "Semiramis." Charents dedicated the book to Laylee.

[2] P. Makintsian was vice chairman of the people's committee in Armenia in 1921. The government responded quickly to Charents' needs at the time.

[3] It was probably the session dedicated to the "crushing of the left front" of the imagists. Apov recalls in his memoirs that Charents was among those shouting in protest. Charents' "proletarian writers": The "Kuznitsa" and similar groups.

Grisha Kegham V. Atamian (b. 1895): A government employee whom Charents first met in 1920. He was attached to the Workers' Committee in Erevan, and was in charge of economic planning in the first weaving factory.

Dear Grisha,

I am writing this letter though I do not know whether it will reach you or whether I will get an answer. Any reply may be sent by means of my courier. Make sure you get the address, and please give him any communication for me.

We are in Moscow, and should have entered the State University, but it has no sleeping quarters, and does not provide board. For that reason we registered temporarily at the Oriental University which offers both.

I'm very interested in what they are saying about me there, and how my work is being received by the Provincial Revolutionary Committee, and what consequences there might have been. I beg you to write me about it in detail because it is a matter that concerns me deeply. It is possible that we may return to Erevan, and it is important for me to know what the disposition is there towards me.

Write to me about who is there at present and in general what is happening. If you are unable to give your letter to my courier, send it through the Armenian Revolutionary Committee, or better yet the Commissariat of External Affairs.

Accept Arpig's and my greetings.

Yours,

Eghishe Charents

Moscow, October 1921

P.S.: Please write. Convey our regards to Vart,[1] Kohar,[2] and to everyone.

---

[1] Nevart Der Krikorian (1901-1941) to whom Charents dedicated the poem, "Your Rosary."

[2] Kohar Malentsian (b. 1901): Charents dedicated "Princess Death" to her and Vart.

Dear, Dear Grisha,

Your letter made me more than happy.

I am very pleased and thankful. If you do not get suddenly lazy, and if you continue to write me such detailed letters frequently, I will regard myself extremely fortunate.

My dear Grisha, you say that you will be coming to Moscow. That is fine. But once you get here, what will you live on? You must be aware that living conditions here are very difficult. First, it is impossible to find a place to stay; and second, at least a million and a half a month is needed to live on. If you are planning to do some kind of work here, that's a different matter. But I do not understand why you wish to come. Moscow is not a "rose-colored" place, no matter how it is visualized there. Especially if one does not have the means. After all my travels and experiences, I have returned to my earlier judgment, that it is not "places" that are in themselves good or bad, but the individual himself, or the people around him.

As Shant has said: "Blessed are those who move in an environment and among people that suit them."[1] That describes it well. Think about it.

Your coming to Moscow will make me personally happy. It will be good to make our way together in the city. But don't look on it as some kind of romantic adventure—it is not that, by any means—at best, it will be difficult and even dull; especially, I repeat, when means are limited and when everything is reduced to a bestial struggle for a piece of bread.

Dear Grisha, if you were to ask me, I would advise you not to come to Moscow, especially since you do not have a definite purpose. You can't study at any university, and it is useless to audit any classes. Though it will make me happy, beyond that there is no purpose whatever. But until you do come, keep writing; the more often you write the better. Your letters console me. Write in detail about everything that is going on, who the young writers are, and what they are doing. In a word, everything. Don't forget to tell me how the people feel about the Soviet regime. This is something that interests me a lot. What are the so-called "Dashnagtsagan intelligentsia" doing, and the non-political intellectuals, the "educators," for example.

Write, and the more the better.

Where is Tavakalian?[2] What is he doing? If you see him, give him my address and ask him to write to me. The same with Apov.[3] I would write to them, but I don't have their addresses.

Greetings to all our friends, to Kohar, Nevart, Arshalooys,[4] and Karnig Kalashian.[5] Tell Karnig that I remember him with joy. I would have written to him, but did not have the time. The courier was in a hurry.

Greetings from Arpig.

> *Yours,*
> *Charents*

Moscow, November 1, 1921

[1] From *The Actress,* a novel by Levon Shant (1869-1951), playwright and novelist.

[2] Menatsakan Tavakalian (1892-1926): Chairman of the Erevan Provincial Revolutionary Council in 1921, Secretary of the Erevan Committee. Charents came to know him in 1920.

[3] Kevork Apov (1897-1965): Poet and writer.

[4] Arshalooys der Hovnanian (1890-1958): Writer and translator; late in life, director of the Armenian section of the copyright bureau.

[5] Karnig Kalashian (1884-1921): A poet whom Charents came to know in 1920, in Erevan.

Dear Levonian,

While your brother[1] was still here in Moscow, he told me that "Kegharvest" had already been printed,[2] except that it did not yet have a jacket. Please, if it is at all possible, send me a copy, even without the jacket, with my courier (Siroosh Hagopian).[3] I am so anxious to have new Armenian books, that a copy will help satisfy my longing for a time.

Mr. Levonian, I apologize again for bothering you so much about the money for my books. At present, my situation has become bearable, so the problem is not an urgent one for the moment.

Perhaps you would be interested to know that my collected works are to be published within two months in two volumes (700-750 pages) by the Soviet Armenian publishing committee.

Accept my warm respects and greetings. Please don't refuse my request.

Yours,
Eghishe Charents

Moscow, January 8, 1922

---

[1] Karekin Levonian had two brothers; the one referred to here was probably Levon Levonian, an engineer-inventor who lived in Tiflis, and was transferred to Moscow in 1930.
[2] Volume VII of the publication which appeared in 1921.
[3] Siroosh Hagopian (b. 1901) was studying economics in Moscow.

Dear Grisha,

I am writing this letter in a hurry, and I urge that you rush to answer it. We are worried because we heard here that Karnig Kalashian has died, and there is no way we can verify the news.

Dear Grisha, as soon as you receive my letter, let me know by telegram. You need only write one word, "yes" or "no," or "it's a lie," and we'll understand.

If you have not forgotten our friendship, you will do this for me. If Karnig is alive, see him and convey my warmest regards; also tell him to write to me; we too shall write. Tell him we have not forgotten him, and that we never shall. If the news is correct (may God prevent it), visit his wife and express our deepest sorrow. Say that Karnig will always be alive for us, as a good friend and Armenian poet, and that his memory will always be bright in the hearts of his friends, and in the hearts of those who love Armenian literature.

Send the wire to the enclosed address.

Accept the friendliest of greetings from Arpig and me. Say hello to all our friends. Write me soon. Special greetings to Apov. Tell him I am fond of him and have not forgotten him. Let him write me through the address of the Armenian Mission.

Yours,
Eghishe Charents

Moscow, January 17, 1922

Dear Grisha:

Many thanks for your last letter. I was deeply moved and gratified. Whatever one may think of him, it was too bad about K. Kalashian. He was a man, after all; he lived in this world; he saw the sun. And he was a writer besides. Whether good or bad, let's leave that aside. It is enough that he felt literature with all his heart, breathed it, lived it.

I remember the great care and tenderness with which he edited his work, arranged it page by page for publication some day . . . but . . . he died, and his papers became orphans, even more so than his children, because in time his children will grow up and manage on their own initiative, while the papers must wait helplessly for someone else's initiative.

You know, Grisha, there is something tragic in the destiny of our generation, especially our literary generation. A great writer like Derian—surely the principal pillar of our post-Toumanian literature—died, and no one seemed to take note of that death, or sense the tragedy of the loss, the gap that was left in our literature afterwards. That's what happened when Derian died;[1] and it seems plain that K. Kalashian's death will attract even less notice. Apparently only personal

friends can feel such losses, and perhaps one or two intellec-
tuals who share the same spiritual temperament, and the same
general fate—and no more. In terrifying days like the ones
we are living now, perhaps we could not reasonably expect
any appreciable attention to be given to the deaths of two
poets. Vahan Derian died at a time when the Dashnagtsagans
ruled the fatherland; they ignored the poet's death because
he was a bolshevik. As for K. Kalashian, the bolsheviks were
in power when he died and they similarly ignored him because
he was Dashnagtsagan. If we poets had any self-respect, we
would long since have abandoned our calling; when the one
thing for which we are able to sacrifice everything, the one
thing which is the essence of our being, is so easily condemned
and denigrated . . . because besides being a poet, we must
also be . . . citizens. You may kill the citizen, if you will, but
for God's sake don't forget the poet. The citizen is for today,
the poet for always. It is possible to kill the citizen, but not
the poet. There are circumstances in which the citizen may
have to be killed, if he is dangerous to the dispositions of the
time; but the poet, if he is an authentic poet and not merely
a "citizen arranging rhymes," will remain of value in the long
run, no matter how dangerous he may appear in the present.
This is the reality, but the present has its own reality, and
"everything is in vain, and metaphysical delirium."[2]

> *Blessed are they who are still to come,*
> *Happier and more joyous than we . . .*
> *Who became strangers in our own land*
> *While you will be masters in our house . . .*[3]

This is how K. Kalashian addressed those who were still
to come. And if they were *not to come* . . . and if there should
not be a "house," what would it matter? If the Turks were
to cross the Arpachay once more, there would be no "house"
left, nor any "future" at all that would "come."

> *Blessed is he who has a native land now . . .*

This is what Derian said in Orenbourg.

Who enters the tomb with peaceful heart,
Blessed is he a thousand times.[4]

V. Derian and K. Kalashian. Two poets. Two citizens. One Dashnagtsagan, the other bolshevik. They might have slain each other on the front, or turned each other in to the Cheka. But how much alike are they in their hearts, in the most intimate depths of their beings. If that "other world" really existed, and if they were to meet each other "there," I know that they would embrace like brothers. They would look upon the distant sufferings of our country with sad eyes and pounding hearts. And together they would cry or rejoice at what sadness or happiness befell it.

Glory to them forever, and blessings on their memory.

This may seem less like a letter than an essay. But then, whenever the heart speaks, the pen cannot fail to respond. The reverse, however, is not always true . . .

My dear Grisha, it is difficult to describe the longing with which I wait for your letters. I do want to come. So very very much. The first volume of my book (320 pages) is already completed. The second volume will be ready by the end of April. I'll come then. I miss the wines of Armenia . . . and not only the wines, but the people, friends, all of them.

Here we are managing somehow. Arpig is studying. I am doing no work at all. I am completely occupied with the publication of my books. There is nothing new of interest to us. There are some new developments in literature, but you can't say anything about them in letters. There are many many names which as yet have little meaning for the unfamiliar reader. I will bring books with me when I come,[5] and we'll talk. One matter concerns me. Where can we stay until we find a room? With you, I suppose. You haven't given up your place? If you can, arrange a place for us even now, and write to me if it is more appropriate for me to file an application here. In any event, please look after this. It keeps worrying me.

Write to me about the political situation there. You don't expect anything to happen in the spring, do you? Address your letter to the Armenian Mission here; it will reach me. I await your letter eagerly; write, dear Grisha, your letters are my only consolation.

Accept my warmest greetings; and regards from Arpig.

Say hello to all my friends; kiss Nevart and Kohar for me. Tell them that in my first book there is a poem, "Princess Death," which is dedicated to them. I have not forgotten them. Let them not forget me.

> *Yours,*
> *Charents*

Moscow, March 20, 1922

[1] Vahan Derian died on January 7, 1920, in Orenbourg. It was not until January 7, 1921, that a memorial tribute was offered in Erevan, through the efforts of Charents.

[2] A Russian proverb.

[3] Quoted from "The Last Girl," a book of quatrains by K. Kalashian (published in Etchmiadzin, 1920).

[4] Quoted from a poem by Vahan Derian, written in 1912. He could not have been in Orenbourg at the time.

[5] Charents returned to Armenia at the end of June 1922.

Mamigon Kevorkian (1879-1962): Director of the State Theater, Secretary of "Nork," playwright, and translator.

Dear Mamigon Kevorkian,

I have already reached Moscow, but things are still uncertain. I don't have a room, the financial situation is unbearable, in a word, everything is miserable. And on top of all this, my heart does not seem to be attached to Moscow this year; now I dream of Nayiri, "Mesopotamia,"[1] and the "flute." Mamigon Kevorkian, write letters! Write whatever you want, but write. What is happening at "Nork?"[2] When will it be out? What sort of materials are being submitted? Did Ashod[3] give an affirmative or, perhaps I should say, practical answer about my being correspondent? When I told Mravian[4] here that I could be a correspondent for "Nork," he said there was no salary for the position, only payment per line for what was published. That would not help me much, because "Nork" may not appear more than once every three months, and I couldn't possibly support two people on what I would earn that way. It would have meant a lot to me to receive 30 to 40 rubles a month, for which I could have not only reported on the local literary scene, but also provided all kinds of material for the paper, as much as they wanted. The only problem is that it has to be put on a regular basis, with a sum given to me every month from the local representative.[5] Talk to Ashod about this; perhaps it can still be arranged. I repeat, if they give me a regular salary, I can contribute a variety of very interesting things. I just can't be made to wait for payment until an issue is published.

There is nothing of great literary interest at the moment. A few books have been published about Einstein, but they are expensive and I can't afford to buy them. There is nothing new on Spengler.[6] If anything turns up, I'll send it along. Perhaps I haven't been able to look around sufficiently yet. If there are any particular books you want, let me know. I'll send them through the mission.

A small collection[7] of my poems is at the press, and will be printed by the end of the month. I'll forward a copy as soon as it is ready.

I am sending you the second volume of my collected works; you'll receive it from Hakhoumian.[8]

Please write to me. About "Nork," about Erevan, about literary events; in a word, about everything. And don't forget to talk to Hovannissian about my request.

Accept my warmest greetings.

Yours,
Eghishe Charents

Moscow, October 1, 1922

[1] In the summer of 1922, C. and M. Kevorkian and D. Hakhoumian used to go swimming in the lake created by the hydroelectric dam on the Hrasdan River; a small island had been formed in the lake which they called "Mesopotamia."
[2] The literary magazine "Nork" was published from 1922 to 1928. Reference is to the first issue, December 1922.
[3] Ashod Hovannissian (1887-1972): A political figure and an editor of "Nork."
[4] Askanaz Mravian (1885-1929) was a prominent Party member, and Minister of Foreign Affairs and of Culture of Armenia.
[5] The Soviet Armenian representative in Moscow beginning in 1921 was Sahag Der Kaprielian (1886-1937), a political leader who was executed during the Stalinist purges of 1937.
[6] M. Kevorkian had asked Charents to look for a book by Spengler (1880-1936). Charents himself was influenced by Spengler.
[7] "Poesozourna," published in Moscow in 1923.
[8] Literary critic Dikran Hakhoumian (1894-1973).

Dikran Shahir, penname of Dikran Hakhoumian (1894-1973): Poet, literary critic. In a book of poems, he refers to himself as Dikran Shahir, the name Charents uses here. Shahir is an Arabic word meaning poet.

Dear Dikran Shahir,

I read your article[1] about me when I was in Tiflis, and it pleased me very much. I was impressed with the "amiable" spirit that marked almost every line of the article. It is very good. I am already back in Moscow, but my heart is no longer happy here; it longs for the shores of the Zankou, and the flute of Nayiri. I wait impatiently for letters. I want you to write often, about Nayiri, about Erevan, about yourself. What is happening in Erevan? When will "Nork" be out. Write, dear Dikran Shahir, about what you are doing, what you are writing, and what expectations you have of the future. I have already turned my "Poesozourna" to the press; it will be about 32 pages, and will be out at the end of this month. You will get a copy when it's printed. My courier will bring you some of my books; please distribute them according to the notes I have written on them. The whole package will be given to you, along with letters for you to distribute.

I am not settled yet in the way I should be; my financial

situation is extremely uncertain; in a word, there is little here to cheer about. New literary directions are almost non-existent. As much as you wish of new publications, but nothing to catch the eye. If I come across anything worthwhile, I will send it along.

Greetings to friends; write soon. The more often you write, the more satisfied I'll be. Greetings to your wife.

Yours,
Charents

Moscow, October 1, 1922

[1] "Eghishe Charents" by Dikran Hakhoumian published in "Soviet Armenia," September 10, 1922.

Dear Shahir,

This is the third letter[1] I am writing to you, though I have had no answers as yet. You could at least have answered my first letter by now, if you had wanted to. Accompanying this letter are eight copies of my "Poesozourna"; please distribute them according to the notes I have attached. Let me know what you think of the book,[2] which I consider my only book, and the *first* after Derian. My opinion—the author's opinion—cannot be worth much in this instance.

I am not sending copies to "Nork" or "Soviet Armenia," because Mamigon, you, Choubar, and Ashod Hovannissian will be getting them. It didn't seem necessary to send them to the editorial offices as well.

I also wanted to send one to Makintsian, but I was told that he was coming to Moscow in the next few days. If he happens to be in Erevan when my books arrive, tell him he was not ignored.

Dear Dikran Shahir, is there anything new in Erevan? I want so much to know what's going on there. I wrote to Mamigon too; not a word yet. I cannot understand this neglect.

Is it only when people meet that they pretend "friendship," perhaps for the sake of courtesy? O dismal misconception. An exalted Derzhavinian[3] style is needed to lyricize such human ingratitude! And you, Brutus, did the sadness of that "farewell flute" fade so quickly in your Nayirian heart? The sound echoes in my consciousness to this day, and will continue that way, until my charred remains are buried, until "my soul of fire goes one night, and rests."[4]

So then, *gloria victis*, dear Hakhoumian, glory to the defeated, and before anyone else to my mocking heart, which was vanquished in the arena of friendship like Don Quixote. O no, I still cannot believe that, dear Shahir, and I know, I feel in my heart that tomorrow or the next day all these unworthy doubts will be submerged in a flood of letters from you, Mamigon and all my good friends.

Accept my best greetings, my best also to your wife. There is no literary news of any importance here.

Yours,
Charents

Moscow, October 28, 1922

[1] According to Hakhoumian, he had two additional letters from Charents, which have not been found. Hakhoumian also tells us that he answered Charents' letters, and remembers the number of letters he wrote [eleven], which apparently were not saved.
[2] Hakhoumian's review of this book appeared in "Baikar," first issue, 1923, under the pen name of H. Nar.
[3] Reference is to the Russian poet G.R. Derzhavin (1743-1816), noted for his full-blown style.
[4] From the first lines of a poem by D. Hakhoumian, "My Soul of Fire Goes."

Dear Mamigon Kevorkian,

This is my third letter to you, with not a single reply. I don't understand what this silence means? Could it be that it was only "Mesopotamia" that made us feel close to each other? I sent you two of my books, my "Poesozourna," and soon you will receive a new poem of mine, "Romance Without

Love."[1] Don't these have any value in your eyes? Well, let it be. Perhaps I too must be formal and speak of "official" things.

There is a problem. I have submitted the first part[2] of my novel to "Nork." Comrade Hovannissian told me that it was already published. I gave him the second part, for which I received an honorarium in Russian currency. I ask that you send me, as soon as it is possible, the remainder of the payment for both parts of the book, less what I have already received. The first part occupied at the minimum two printed issues, the second will occupy about three, making five in all, for which I should receive 250 rubles in gold. Subtract from this sum what I have received, and send the balance as quickly as you can, care of the mission. I intend to come to Erevan at the end of January,[3] but even that depends on my receiving this money. So to conclude the "practical" part of my letter, I ask that you forward the funds soon, since I will be unable to travel without them, nor even continue work on my novel, in which "Nork" surely has a stake.

How many times have I written and inquired about "Nork"—with no response. Scores of friends come from Erevan every day. Is it very difficult to send a letter with one of them? Please, dear Mamigon, write to me when our "Nork" will finally appear, which I am afraid will be so late that it will be an autumn planting!

Also, my "noble knight," which issue is it to appear in?[4] Ashod was saying that it will not be in the first issue. Will it then be in the second? I think that as the author I have a right to inquire about this officially, if you hesitate to tell me as a friend.

In a word, I hope that as soon as this letter reaches its destination, you will send me (1) a long letter in reply, (2) my honorarium, and (3) the issue of "Nork," in anticipation of which "my eyes have become water." In any event, I will have to remain here until I receive the money from you, so don't forget to send me the "Nork." I think, from what Ashod said, I should receive it by January 1, or at the very latest by the 15th.

Accept my respects and greetings; and greetings to Sarian, Kalantar, Misha Manuelian,[5] and all my friends. My wife sends her greetings as well.

Yours,
Eghishe Charents

Moscow, December 20, 1922

P.S.: Anything new in Erevan? Would it have been so hard for you to send a couple of bottles of cognac with Ashod? They would have been more than welcome in this cold city. Ah, worthless people, and worse, undependable friends! Garen Mikaelian is here; we meet every day and remember you and talk about you. We don't let our friends down. I'll come. I'll be in Erevan one day and woe to you, Mamigon Kevorkian, who so quickly forget your friends. Life is interesting here, especially the theater; and most of all the staging of "Turandot" and "The Death of Tarelkin" by Vakhtangov and Meyerhold.[6] Things seem to be happening in literature too. There are enough books about Spengler; I won't go back on my word. If you want any book, write me; I'll send whatever you want.

Once more, accept my greetings.

Yours,
Charents

---

[1] "Romance Without Love" was published in Moscow, December 1922.
[2] The first part of Charents' novel *Erkir Nayiri* (Land of Nayiri) appeared in the first issue of "Nork"; the second part was published in volume II, 1923.
[3] Charents left Moscow on January 1, 1923, stayed in Tiflis a short time, and reached Erevan on January 16 or 17.
[4] Published in the second issue of "Nork."
[5] The painter Martiros Sarian (1880-1972); film director L. Kalantar (1882-1959); and actor-writer M. Manuelian (1877-1944).
[6] Vakhtangov directed "Turandot" by Cozzi (1722-1806); and Meyerhold staged "The Death of Tarelkin" by Sukhovo-Kopilin (1817-1903); both in Moscow in 1922.

My very dear Hov. Toumanian,

    I deeply regret that I will not have the opportunity to visit you,[1] and personally convey my high esteem to our most beloved poet, to the greatest master of our language. At four o'clock today, I am going to Erevan with Alexandre Fedorovich.[2] I am going to our own land profoundly convinced that only there on our native soil will we be able to create our own culture, our literature, which must derive from your creativity, as an indigenous creative tradition. But I leave with grievous disappointment, sad that I will not be near you during your convalescence, the convalescence of the patriarch of the Nayirian language, from whom our native land still harbors abundant and wondrous expectations.

    Dear Toumanian, I have a strong belief that you will recover, to give us more of your "Glittering Nightingale," about which I had heard as a child; I still wait expectantly for its completion. Accept your youngest pupil's warmest regards, and know that in Erevan I will impatiently await your return. I will be happy to come to Tiflis to offer my boundless reverence for a life so full of wisdom and achievement, which lavished such spiritual and cultural treasures on our people.

    Again and again, I wish you complete recovery, and kiss your deserving hand.

Yours,
Eghishe Charents

Moscow, January 1, 1923

---

[1] Charents wrote this letter when Toumanian was in a Moscow hospital, suffering from cancer. It is possible that Charents was among the Armenian intellectuals, led by Sahag Der Kaprielian, who met Toumanian at the Kursk station when he was transferred to Moscow towards the end of December 1922. According to Toumanian's daughter, Nevart, Charents first met her father in the summer of 1921.

[2] Alexandre Fedorovich Miasnikian, who was devoted to Toumanian, probably prompted Charents to write this letter.

Garen Mikaelian (1883-1941): A writer who lived in Moscow. Charents came to know him well in 1921-1922.

Dear Garen,

I just received your second letter, and it made me very happy. I am grateful for your considerate attention. But it is not fair to reproach me. I had sent a letter with Dikran Mousheghian,[1] and I am writing another now. The "Nork" issue has already been sent to the mission, and perhaps you have seen it. By the end of this month, perhaps sooner, the second issue will come out; and this time I will send you a copy myself immediately.

Briussov's translation[2] pleased me very much. I am grateful to you. If it is not going to be published soon, please send me the manuscript or a copy typed on a Remington.

Here the days are getting warmer. I'm glad, and glad too that I have come. Man does not live by the word alone; he must have bread as well! You will do well to come this summer. Our Nayirian sun is everything they say it is.

Dear Garen, it will please me if you write often. And something about the literary life there. It is good here, intimate, but provincial. I would like to go to Petersburg and settle there. I don't regret my return, but I have no desire to stay. Still I don't think it is possible to leave before September.

I am writing the third part of my novel, *Nayiri*.[3] The second part will appear in "Nork's" next issue. You have probably read the first part. I would be interested in your opinion. How is your *Pakin*[4] doing? Have you finished it? What else are you writing?

I hope you keep me informed about what's happening there, and about your literary plans. Do not forget, Garen. I remember our meetings with great satisfaction and I wish that until we meet again our "good neighborly relations" may be sustained in letters.

Accept my greetings, and convey them to your Arpenig

Avedovna. My Arpenig Avedovna sends her greetings.

Yours,

Charents

Erevan, March 10, 1923

P.S.: Don't forget to send the translation, even if it is in manuscript form. We can have it printed here. So, dear Garen, send it soon.

Now about our life here. There is no literary news, except for "Nork." "Mourj"[5] has also come out, and you can get a good idea about it by examining the replica[6] of it issued under your very nose. Do you understand what I am referring to, the local group there? The reputation it has gained here, disgust and outrage, is fully deserved.

"Baikar," the supplement of "Soviet Armenia," is being published. It's not much. There are two good talents in the theater, Aroos Voskanian[7] and V. Papazian,[8] who breathe some spirit into our existence here.

I had finished the letter when Mamigon brought the issue of "Nork," so I am sending it along.

Please accept it; Mamigon asks that payment for it be made to the "Nork" editorial office, whenever it is convenient.

E. Char.

---

[1] Dikran Mousheghian (1886-1935): A political figure.

[2] Valery Briussov translated Charents' "Poems for All" in January-February of 1923. It was not published. In his memoirs, the architect M. Mazmanian recalls that Charents did not like the translation and would not approve its publication. Later, according to I. Postupalsky, the translation was reworked and approved, and was eventually published. The Briussov translation was included in a volume of Charents' collected works published in Moscow in 1956.

[3] The novel was finished in August 1924.

[4] Reference is to Mikaelian's *Lotee Pakin*, a dramatic study, on which he worked a long time.

[5] "Mourj" (Hammer), a literary magazine devoted to proletarian literature, published in 1922-1923, and edited by Azad Veshdooni.

[6] The replica referred to is the monthly "Kura," and the group, the Armenian Society of Literature in Moscow.

[7] Aroos Voskanian (1889-1943) was an actress.
[8] Vahram Papazian (1888-1968) was an actor and author.

Dear Mamigon,

Epistle I

Has it been ordained from above that I, the wanderer, have been destined to remain without news, and be kept out of contact from the life there? And who is it, who is the one responsible for this, if not Prince Mamkoon himself, from whom I have received a mere note consisting of nine points, each of which could be the subject of a long letter, while the last ("To write a long letter"), the expression of hope and good news!

Dear Mamkoon,[1] I say all this only because I have not, since leaving Armenia, received any letters from anyone, and have written to no one (except the one to you). It must be understood by you, the prince, what joy your letter can bring to me, the poet, including as it surely will so many interesting things. Dear Mamkoon, listen to my supplications and write, about yourself, the State Theater,[2] "Nork," about literary events, about anything you wish. And this pen of mine is witness that for every word you write me, God—or even I, if you so desire—will reward you with letters and books, with whatever you may wish.

Epistle II

"Nork" before everything else. What's going on there? Will it come out or not? I am curious about the contents. Then the State Theater of course. What plans does it have? You had written that my *kabkaz*[3] would be staged in December. Did it fall through, or will it yet see the light? What are the Nayirian literati doing there? Your views of our contemporary literary reality are of interest to me. Comrade Garinian[4] is here; according to him, it is a desert, a dead place, a white nirvana.

If my humble life interests you, I must say that I have never been so unproductive as now. I don't know whether it is a crisis or simply the end. Not a single idea, nor anything resembling an idea, sullies the purity, or rather the emptiness, of my imagination. Now my imagination is in turn a sky without clouds, a night without dawn. I know the reason. Last winter Erevan performed a massive job on the twisting road of my spiritual progress. It tore from within me everything that was Nayirian, romantic, indigenous. As if it had all been written with chalk on the blackboard of my soul . . .

Epistle III

And so one winter a fateful hand wiped all that away with the sponge of time, and in its place left an empty space. I was happy for it. That romanticism had a way of evoking the child-like. So I am grateful to the Erevan of 1923. The problem is that the "empty space" has not been filled. Will it be, when and with what? The poet in me does not know. But one thing seems very plain: whatever new seeds finally fertilize my spirit, now delivered of its Nayirian romanticism, the harvest will be higher, fuller, and riper than before. Whatever its character, romanticism is puerile, an identification of the young, much like religion is of people generally; or perhaps the contrary, an evocation of old age and the sunset it suggests (in the last analysis it may be the same thing, children and the elderly differing very little in their souls). So, dear Mamkoon, may the concrete, positive approach to life flourish, an approach that is serious, as every mature person should be, if he feels healthy and vigorous, and part of the triumphant class that is on its way up.

Epistle IV and Last

It should be clear from what I have said why I cannot go on with *Erkir Nayiri*. Its time has passed. I am far from all that, and taking shape before me, perhaps barely emerging from the mist, is the palpable countenance of all humanity, today's form, and tomorrow's way of life (Soviet regime plus Americanism). It is there that the new impulses, if that is destined to be, will relate to my creative energies.

Let us finish with this. I am bored in Moscow, but I don't

want to come to Armenia. I would like to go to Europe, to
America, to see with my own eyes the culture that is called
machinism and technocracy, about which "Lef"[5] writes with
such inept immaturity, and Wells[6] with such ingenuity.

This ends my letter. Dear Mamkoon, write. If this letter
remains unanswered too, it will mean that still another tradi-
tion of *Erkir Nayiri* has been severed: Not to write to a fellow
Nayirtsi, and not even to expect a letter.

Greetings from Arpig and me.

Yours,

Charents

Moscow, February 2, 1924

[1] A familiar form of Mamigon. The use of "prince" is an allusion to one
of the great Armenian dynasties, the Mamigonians.
[2] Besides being secretary of "Nork," Mamigon Kevorkian was also director
of the State Theater.
[3] It was not staged in Erevan at that time.
[4] Reference is to literary critic and statesman Ardashes Garinian (b. 1886).
[5] Charents' debt to Constructivism is evident here. In Russia the literary
school following its precepts was formed in 1923 by the poets I. Selvinsky
and A. Chicherin, and lasted until 1930. "Lef" also largely defended its ap-
proach (Mayakovsky, Meyerhold, etc.), as did the ill-fated "Standard" which
Charents edited. Only one issue was printed, and that one not distributed
on Miasnikian's order.
[6] Charents' *I and Ilyitch* was influenced by Wells' *The Time Machine*. Charents
was fascinated with work of this kind, but shook off those influences when
he returned from abroad.

*Alexandre Fedorovich Miasnikian (1886-1925): An eminent Soviet political and
military figure.*

(To A. Miasnikian)

The artist Garo Halabian[1] has sculpted a bust of Lenin,
one and a half to two times larger than life. In the opinion
of some friends, and mine too, the bust is quite successful;
it can even be said that among those we have seen, it

resembles him most. He has prepared the sculpture from clay, then casting it in gypsum or bronze, whatever is considered appropriate. Some Transcaucasian institution should order the work, the Transcaucasian Committee, for example. Sahag[2] is thinking of acquiring it for the Transcaucasian and Armenian missions, but that of course will not mean as much to the sculptor, from the point of view of prestige, as would an order from the central committee of Transcaucasia; and the work, I strongly believe, is worthy of that. In a word, if you like the idea, you can write or wire Sahag, and ask for a photo of the work (Halabian himself can't do that since a special photographer is required), on the basis of which you can decide to accept or reject the work, according to your judgment of its value.

Accept my communist greetings.

Yours,

Charents

Moscow, March 8, 1924

[1] Though Charents had met Halabian in 1921, they became good friends in 1923. In 1924, Halabian was studying at the Art institute of Moscow.
[2] Sahag Der Kaprielian was Moscow representative of the Transcaucasian Federation.

Dear Alexandre Fedorovich,

I have been in Erevan for two months now, at the disposition of the Erevan party committee.[1] Things are going well, the work interests me, but September is approaching and I must decide what I should do next. As I told you in Moscow,[2] my wish is to go abroad,[3] and all my hopes to that end rest only on what you may be willing to do for me. I don't expect much from Erevan despite my belief that comrade Ashod Hovannissian[4] is also well disposed towards me. I don't think that he can by himself succeed at the Cheka in arranging a trip abroad for me, with all its financial considerations. In a word, my hope is on you alone, and I think that if I am ever going to realize this wish which I have felt for so long, it can only be with your help.

I would like to go abroad in October, for five or six months, preferably by way of Germany,[5] and from there, if possible, to all the European centers and then to North America. I may be able to give some lectures[6] in Armenian communities about our cultural life in Armenia, especially about modern literature. One of the reasons for making my request early is that, if approval is granted, I will have time to collect materials (statistics and other facts about the educational, industrial and other aspects of life in Armenia), materials that can be useful in the lectures I mentioned.

If I am unable to go abroad, I am thinking of returning to Moscow at the beginning of September, and settling there for good, hoping that the central committee of the People's Commissariat of Culture will give me some kind of work in the Moscow section of the State Press of Armenia, or in another establishment.

Such are my plans for the future. I am putting myself completely in your hands. I wait for your answer.

Accept my deep respects and party greetings.

Yours,

Eghishe Charents

Erevan, August 3, 1924

[1] On the suggestion of the Erevan party committee, Charents undertook an investigation of village life in July 1924, as a result of which he wrote "In the Village of Priguns."

[2] Charents had met Miasnikian in Moscow in June and July of 1924.

[3] Charents' wish to go abroad was first made known in a letter (May 14, 1924) from the critic H. Sourkhatian to Miasnikian: "I'm sending you Charents' letter. Read it. I will get it back later. He is our finest talent, and it is necessary to send him to Europe for a trip to see the world. No one is left of our new Russian poets who has not been abroad. Isn't Charents worthy of that? He will see a great deal, and be able to write a great deal. Perhaps you can do something in Moscow. Let him go for a trip until

autumn. We will not often have a talent of such proportions. Charents is a poet of world stature."

[4] The historian, Ashod Hovannissian, was secretary of the central committee in Erevan in 1924.

[5] Charents went abroad by way of Turkey and returned through Germany.

[6] As far as is known, Charents did not give any lectures to Armenian communities abroad.

Ashod Hovannissian (1887-1972): Historian and political figure who, together with Paul Makintsian (1884-1937) and A. Mravian, edited "Nork."

Dear Ashod Hovannissian,

I have finished my business here, received my papers, and am going to Moscow. From there it looks as if I will be going abroad.[1] My early departure from Moscow depends on the visa, that is, on Sahag.[2] The sooner he gets it, the sooner I will go. My itinerary is approximately this: Moscow, Berlin, Paris, London, New York, with two or three months in America, then back to Spain, Italy, Istanbul, and Batum.[3]

This is my plan and I hope I have the opportunity to accomplish it.

I intend to publish *Erkir Nayiri* in America. If you definitely agree to write an introduction,[4] it will be best to get it to me before I go to Moscow. Sending it to me later will be difficult; I am afraid it will never reach me. Without an introduction, I would hesitate to publish *Nayiri* abroad because without it the book will hardly serve the purpose intended for its appearance there. Just a few words about revisions I plan to make in *Nayiri*.[5]

The first and most important is in the story of Mr. Maroukeh. In the first part of the novel he is a drunken provincial teacher, beats children, and so on; in the second part he is an unprincipled opponent of Dashnagtsoutioun; and in the third, a bolshevik. This awkward development, as well as some other infelicities, resulted from the fact that I wrote the novel with long interruptions, and had sections published separately. For the second edition, I am doing extensive rewriting, condensing some parts, adding new episodes, expanding some of the actions of the bolsheviks. In a word, I hope that with these changes, my novel will amount to something.

It would be helpful if you could write to me your suggestions about what areas need attention. If only you have the time, and can devote a couple of nights to such work.

I do hope you write the introduction; if you are unable to have it by the time I leave for Moscow, it may be possible to send it through Sahag.

Accept my greetings and friendly respects.

> *Yours,*
> *Charents*

Tiflis, September 13, 1924

---

[1] He left from Batum on November 21, 1924.
[2] Sahag Der Kaprielian.
[3] Just the opposite happened; he left from Batum, and returned through Berlin.
[4] Hovannissian did not write the introduction to the novel.
[5] Actually, only minor revisions were made, concerning the character of Mr. Maroukeh.

Most respected Alexandre Fedorovich,

Before anything else, allow me to express my deepest thanks to you for giving me the opportunity to travel abroad. Allow me further to inform you of what I have done, and what I intend to do.

I have been waiting here for more than a month to get the visa for America. I have thus far been unable to obtain it, and have no hope that waiting any longer will change anything. So I decided to discard the idea of going to America, and instead confine my trip to Europe. I will leave here tomorrow for Athens, then to Rome. I'll visit various Italian cities, and go on to Paris, London, Berlin, Vienna, and back to Moscow.[1] That is my plan. Whether it succeeds or not depends on the offices that have been endowed with the divine right of issuing visas! They have frustrated me from the start. First I went to Moscow where I had to stay a month, only to return to Tiflis; and then another month here. And the consequence of all this? From the sum of 2,000 rubles which I had received, only about a third is left. I was forced to ask for additional money, and was elated when it was granted.

As soon as I reached Istanbul, I wanted to arrange a couple of lectures, but Shahverdian[2] advised against it. "No one will come," he said, explaining that there was no intellectual class, as we understand it, which would be interested in the cultural life of Soviet Armenia. I agreed with him. I soon became aware that there is literally no public life here (I refer to the Armenian community). Only Dashnagtsagans move a bit on the public level, but they too endure a wretched, shadowy existence. Last year, when I read Paul Makintsian's artcles,[3] I thought he was exaggerating the conditions here; now I am convinced it was not an exaggeration at all; if anything, he minimized it, and considerably. It is hard to imagine how pitiable the life of the Armenian community is here. People simply drag out a hapless, miserable life, trying to please the government as much as they can, cringing, acting guilty and defensive, while the government, the Turkish public, the press, etc., endeavor to confine them in an environment of such contempt, judicial terror, and provocation, as to make, the saying goes, a man's hair stand on end. No wonder Armenians have lost even the basic elements of communal life. There are no meetings, no lectures; it is futile even to mention party organizations. I met with a group of "intellectuals" here, all meek and subdued specters whose eyes glistened with terror and servility, pleading, always pleading. When I first arrived, the editors of a couple newspapers came to meet me, and asked such idiotic questions that I did not know what to say to them. For example, the editor of "Nor Loor"[4] asked if Mr. Miasnikov was Armenian, or merely pretended to be. Or, are there Armenians in Russia in high government posts? And they went on and on in this manner. Mr. Makintsian occupied a select place in the interest of these honorable editors. What does he do? Is he still in his post? Is he generally respected? Etc., etc., etc. What astonished me most was that those gentlemen, who call themselves editors (!!!), do not have the most elementary idea about the structure of the Soviet regime. They have no understanding of what the central executive committee is, or of any similarly basic reality. I gave some information to two such "editors" who came to see me, but only "Jamanag" printed a small part of my interview, and that with many mistakes. As for "Nor Loor" and "Avedis," they had informed Shahverdian that they could not unfortunately "adorn their pages" with my interview because . . . the police had forbidden it. In a word they looked on me here as a "bolshevik agent," and I felt proud about that.

Of course I announce everywhere and to everybody that I am traveling as a writer and have no "mission," and that I have not been dispatched by any official body. But they don't believe it. It seems that it is not, as is generally felt, the "ghost of communism" that hovers over Europe, but the terror of communism. There is so much fear of bolshevism in these countries that it is impossible to describe. In the smallest movements, in the most insignificant disturbances, the finger of bolsheviks is discerned, and loud alarms sounded, to alert the leadership. The terrified bourgeois, like a stunned ox, eyes filled with blood, sees the color red in everything, shrieks with fear and sounds new alarms. And it is these alarms that have driven Mr. Chamberlain and his friends to seek the formation of a "front" against the bolshevik danger. Exposed to this environment, observing the life of the "universal bourgeois," my heart swells with pride that I am a bolshevik, and a member of the Leninist system.

As to my literary work, I hope it will not prove disappointing, that I will be redeemed by it. I am thinking of writing a novel,[5] in which I will depict the people abroad from our view-point. I have written a series of poems,[6] two of which I sent to "Soviet Armenia"; and another, titled "Istanbul," I had printed separately, and have sent a copy to you. I would be interested in your opinion of it. I want to publish *Erkir Nayiri* either in Vienna or Paris,[7] but I don't dare do so without an introduction. I inquired about this in a letter I wrote to Makint-sian, but I have not received an answer. If you write[8] to me care of Shahverdian, the letter will reach me, and I would be very thankful.

Accept my deep respects.

With party greetings,
Yours,
Charents

Istanbul, January 8, 1925

P.S.: I also wanted to let you know that I have generally kept away from the Armenian community here, and haven't had anything to do with the so-called "national intelligentsia." I have also abstained from any kind of alcohol, with the grief of the scandal in Tiflis[9] still on my mind, the consequences of which will, I am afraid, be expressed by the party in an appropriate way, after my return.

[1] Of the cities he enumerates, Charents did not visit London and Vienna.
[2] Reference is to Daniel Shahverdian (1882-1938), diplomat, representative of Armenia in Istanbul; he was occupied with the work of repatriating Armenians in the diaspora.
[3] Makintsian's articles "A Year in Istanbul," which appeared in "Mardagoch," Nos. 89-91, 1924.
[4] "Nor Loor" was a political business daily, 1924-1931.
[5] Charents did not write such a novel.
[6] "To Istanbul," "Lenin and Ali," "Istanbul."
[7] *Erkir Nayiri* was not published abroad.
[8] As far as is known, Miasnikian did not write the introduction. He died soon after in an airplane accident. It is widely believed that the crash was not an accident, and that Miasnikian was one of Stalin's early victims.
[9] In the Tiflis incident (recalled by Mahari in his memoirs), Charents was late for an appointment with Miasnikian on the eve of his departure, because he was drinking with Mahari.

Terenig Temirjian (1877-1956): Novelist, poet, and playwright.

Dear Terenig,

Apart from the formal application, I am writing for a special reason. The paper, and particularly the journal,[1] being published in Paris, must be where those writers in Armenia and outside who are committed to the idea of Soviet Armenia, must come together. The chief condition for achieving this is the vigorous support of our writers there, without which hardly anything will be possible. Especially important is the participation of writers who are not party members, and who are familiar with the diaspora.[2] In this respect your own contribution is essential. I hope you won't spare any effort, and will contribute enthusiastically both to our paper and to the journal. It would be good to have short stories and essays about the new life in Soviet Armenia, like the ones occasionally published in "Soviet Armenia." We would also like to have articles about the literary-cultural scene there.

In a word, I hope you will get to work on this quickly and energetically. Now for some news that might interest you.

I met Issahakian[3] in Venice. We were together for a month, and remembered you every day. He is a very pleasant man. He is busy writing "Oosta Karo" which, if it is anything like his description of it, will be a fabulous work. But I am afraid he can tell a story better than he can write one. Anyway, we'll see when he finishes the work. He asked me to send you his greetings; accept this as such. I told him of my delight with your "Judgment," "Nazar the Brave," and other writings. He has not read "Judgment," and read only the last section of "Nazar the Brave"—in a textbook—which he admired very much. I told him of my own feelings as well since I was the first to read and praise your "Nazar the Brave," if you remember.[4]

Well, dear Terenig, how are you? What are you doing? Have you written anything recently? What do you plan for the future? I would like very much for us to write each other regularly. Let this serve as the prologue of such a correspondence; it remains for you to sustain the rhythm.

I liked Venice, Istanbul and Paris very much. Rome and Berlin did not make a particular impression on me. Naples was exceptionally beautiful, as were the island of Capri, Vesuvius, and Pompei. They are unequalled, legendary beauties.

Please be content with this much for now. I wait for your letter and materials. Please write me in detail about the literary-cultural life there.

Accept my greetings, and share them with your family, and kiss your child for me.

Yours,

Charents

Paris, May 7, 1925[5]

---

[1] Charents had the mission to start publication of a journal in Paris with the aim of acquainting the diaspora with the achievements of Soviet Armenia. The project did not succeed. Instead a paper, "Erevan," published three times a week, was initiated in 1925, with journalist Eghia Choubar (1897-1937) sent to edit it.

[2] Temirjian studied in Geneva from 1905 to 1909.

[3] Avetik Issahakian (1875-1957), poet and novelist, was affectionately referred to as "master" in the last years of his life.

[4] Temirjian finished the comedy, "Nazar the Brave," in the fall of 1922. Charents could have read it in January 1923 in Tiflis, or later in Erevan, in the editorial office of "Nork." Charents had met Temirjian in Erevan in 1920.

[5] In Paris, Charents stayed with Simon Priumian, commercial attache of the Transcaucasian Republics and representative of Soviet Armenia in Paris in 1925.

H. Sourkhatian (1882-1938): A distinguished literary critic who wrote the first long and detailed monograph (never published) on Charents' work. He criticized the positions taken by the "Declaration of the Three." Charents accepted some of his strictures and attempted to adjust his views accordingly. Sourkhatian was a victim of Stalin's purges.

(Written from abroad to H. Sourkhatian)

I am abroad. I must emphasize that what we describe as "abroad" is something the like of which we have not seen, not even in pre-revolutionary Russia—the boundless kingdom of the gilded bourgeois, which has achieved a perfection of its kind. Visualize all sorts of things, articles, property—magnificent hotels, shop windows, theaters, shops, mannequins, women, lackeys, journalists, priests, mullahs, diplomats, writers, newspapers, books, cars, beasts—and squatting on them all a thick-necked being who rules, devours, dominates. Everyone cringes before this supreme master, the universal bourgeoisie, who resides in beautiful hotels, eats oysters, and dances the foxtrot. This of course is the first general impression, which immediately overwhelms the observer, but soon the eye gets accustomed to it, and one gets to see more objectively, and discern various aspects of the picture. First of all the high standard of this material culture evokes admiration, a standard which makes our country seem still relatively provincial. It is necessary to acknowledge that this corpulent degenerate, the international bourgeois, required hundreds of years to develop such a material culture; if we were able to separate that creature, now a parasite, from the body, life would become a paradise. A vast material culture has been created here in Europe. One is amazed by its glitter and conveniences, but when one examines it, comes into actual contact with it, one soon realizes that the only beneficiaries are the bourgeois, degenerating and impeding the further progress of that culture, and one must feel at the very least that he must turn communist, if he has not already done so. Do you know what pride is stirred in me by the thought that I am a communist, a bolshevik member of the Leninist establishment? The name alone strikes terror in every educated bourgeois. There is such dread, such animal terror of bolshevism, as to be beyond description. The presence of bolshevism is sensed at almost every turn, and certainly not as a "specter," but as a terrifying (for the bourgeois, of course)

reality, which is moving and gathering force, like a flood of molten iron, to sweep the parasites, the bloated bourgeoisie, off the face of the earth. It senses instinctively the imminence of its demise, but is reluctant to accept it; and with the last exertion of a dying creature enlists various Chamberlains and Mussolinis, who are unlikely to save him.
1925

[1] Published in "Mardagoch," February 18, 1928, under the title of "Fleeting Impressions." There was no date or mention of the person to whom the letter was addressed. According to A.K. Zakarian, one of the editors of Charents' complete works (Erevan, 1967, Vol. VI), the letter could have been addressed to H. Sourkhatian, because Sourkhatian's wife recalled it as part of a ten-page letter Charents wrote from Istanbul, which was lost in 1938. The editor identifies it as having been written from Italy.

(Excerpts from a letter to H. Sourkhatian)[1]
    . . . The mistake, the reason for the mistake lies in these two misunderstandings. The first is that we had no more than a rudimentary idea about life and man generally, and about the proletarian and his life especially. We were over-simplifying everything, making everything seem ordinary, vulgarizing Marx's basic principles. My most urgent conclusion from this: At present we must establish a single criterion for our approach to art: ideological. The rest is detail, a subjective question of "talent," nothing more. This thesis, with all its implications, is new for me, of course, though not for you, because until now we were approaching it from exactly the opposite direction: First art, then ideology. We were giving primacy to art . . .
    While examining art from the Egyptians to the French Impressionists, I felt with all my being that all of it belonged to the same school, and in their time they did; that is the psychology of the ruling class of each era. In that is everything.

. . . Each stroke of those geniuses, each color, mark, is immersed in the psychology of the ruling class of the time, baked in it, so "organically" that you cannot discern where in those works the "class" ends and the "universal" begins . . .

And now it is time we readjusted our viewpoint.

. . . There is no "artistic viewpoint," but there is a proletarian viewpoint. And if we should approach all problems from this and only this viewpoint, we will be spared such misunderstandings as the separation of the art of the same class into different categories, "denying art," or transforming man into a scarecrow of "class advantage." It is necessary to be drenched, baked, and burnt with class psychology, so that each vein, fiber, cell, is tense with the will of victory and dominance; and if you have some talent as a writer, you will be the authentic exponent of your class.

1925

[1] This letter is from H. Sourkhatian's book, *Post-Revolutionary Armenian Literature,* Erevan, 1929. Sourkhatian had excerpted the section translated here. It appears to have been written from Berlin, where Charents was in mid-April, 1925.

To the Editor of "Vishka,"[1]

. . . Now let's go on to other matters.

Dear Souren, your articles[2] gave me the greatest of pleasure, and encouragement comparable to the warm interest shown in my work by the Baku proletariat.[3] Please express my deepest gratitude to the Armenian proletariat of Baku, for the supreme confidence felt in my work. Tell them that their fervent support will be a new and inexhaustible source of inspiration and will impel me to direct all my strength, abilities, and impulses in channels that in the future will enable me to enjoy the vital blessings of their appreciation. Please tell them finally that for a working class to regard a writer in this way is the most enviable fortune that can befall him. Let them accept my warmest greetings from the capitalistic west, where the red specter of communism has already taken form in red organizations, and in the most difficult circumstances endeavors to follow its older friend, the proletariat of the Great Soviet Federation, that huge avant-garde of the international communist revolution, one of the leading regiments of which is the Baku proletariat.

My deepest thanks and warmest greetings.

Now dear Souren, a few words about my thoughts and work here. Let me say before anything else that this trip abroad has worked a fundamental change in me. There, I was a writer first and then a proletarian; here that order has been reversed, and I became a proletarian first, and then a writer. I must say that even while still there, especially after "Standard," this process had already begun in me, but it could hardly have taken its full course there, which it achieved only thanks to my trip abroad. There one becomes so accustomed to the accomplishments of the revolution that soon they are unnoticed like the air around us. It was necessary to live for a time "outside the red line" to be aware of the huge contrast between us and the old world. It was that contrast that impelled me toward certain re-evaluations, and for me such altogether unexpected conclusions, which might have seemed like "provocations" there, created especially for us. What could the reason be, I wondered, that notwithstanding the singular character of the proletarian ideology, in all aspects of life, everywhere, on all horizons without exceptions, the ideology in art and literature has been and is subjected to various divisions and qualifications and very often to contradictory interpretations, like the so-called academic literature and art hung around the neck of the proletariat. When I considered the issue for the first time here in the bourgeois world, where the struggle is so intense, where the mobilization and conservation of strength is so essential, our old "positions" seemed so unsophisticated, wrong and vulgar that I was astonished, that how until today we somehow failed to understand that a fundamental con-

tradiction exists, a vital misunderstanding. To put the ques-
tion in the right perspective is almost to resolve it. And it was
resolved for me in an extremely simple and ordinary way:
I understood, felt in a way that approached elemental simplici-
ty, that the only reason for the basic mistake has been that
the world of art has always been devoid of men made of the
"flesh and bone" of the proletariat. That is the substance
of it. At the same time we ourselves have been apart from
them, and have been "artists" first, and then "proletarians."
We must be especially conscious of this, and straighten our
weakened back, strained by intellectual conceptions, traditions
and psychology. I have said as much to Garo too, and to
Mikael Mazmanian[4] and other friends.[5] We can accomplish
this in only one way; we must once and for all stay away from
all kinds of "isms" which stress the primacy of form, and seek
to be immersed from "head to foot" in proletarian ideology,
understanding that there can be no "artistic," "futuristic,"
"constructivist" or other viewpoint for someone speaking in
the name of the proletariat, but the one and unifying pro-
letarian viewpoint. No other specifications. To learn
everything, approach art and literature, before everything else,
from the viewpoint of the class struggle of the proletariat in
its ultimate victory and universal supremacy. That is the fun-
damental requisite. The rest—form and appearance—is detail,
a minor detail which can only interest the specialist, nothing
more. I became convinced of this while viewing the greatest
works of the so-called "old" art. I felt deeply that all, from
Egyptian sculpture to the French Impressionists, without ex-
ception, belonged to one school, and were dominated by the
mentality of the ruling class of their respective eras. Every
line, color, tint, is touched with that mentality; it is flesh and
body. Their expressions are such as to leave uncertain where
"class" ends and "the universal" begins, where the "class con-
tent" ends, and the "universal form" begins. In this is the most
powerful aspect of that art, from this their most effective in-
fluence, elemental even, which one cannot even understand. It

is what the proletariat requires if it is to extend spiritual in-
fluence over all mankind. As for us, what are we to do? We
thought we could dominate the world with placards and pitiful
polemical plays, whose impact can hardly exceed that of tran-
sitory advertisements. And we considered that the authentic
art of the proletariat. And do you know why we thought so?
Because with our feeble intellectual equipment, we were turn-
ing real workers into lifeless caricatures, ostensibly for "class
advantage," and advantage with little connection to man
himself, but dangling meaninglessly in air. Had we not
"denied" a way of life and a psychology?[6] And the counterfeit
intellectual coin borrowed from Lef was being represented
as the authentic proletarian ideology, as—let it be said—"Marx-
ism," whereas it is nothing but bourgeois materialism of the
hardest kind, nihilism subjected to vulgarity and
Pissarevchina.[7] At last!

A word about my literary work. I have written a long
poem, *Mur des Federes* ("The Wall of the Communists in
Paris"), consisting of three parts—the wall, the city below, and
we shall yet come. It is a long work, about 100 pages. I have
dedicated it to the memory of A. Miasnikian. I hope I have
succeeded in creating something worthy of his memory. I have
also written a number of shorter poems, a few about Lenin,
one a children's poem called "Uncle Lenin." I may publish
three of these in Berlin,[8] if it proves possible.

Ah, dear Souren, I think I have written enough. Now it
is up to you . . .
Berlin, May 14, 1925

[1] This letter was published in "Vishka" (June 1925, No. 1), edited by E.
Souren (Erzenkian), a literary critic. The paper was published in Baku.
[2] Erzenkian published a series of articles on Charents at the time.
[3] Reference is to the broad interest shown in Charents between February
22 and March 7, 1925, when special events were organized in his honor,
and widely reported in the press.
[4] The architects Garo Halabian and Mikael Mazmanian.
[5] Charents had written a similar letter to H. Sourkhatian.

[6] The viewpoint being "denied" here is clearly enunciated in "About the Literary Plan of the 'Standard.'"
[7] Reference is to the Russian critic D. Pissarev (1840-1868) whose views on literary efficacy led him to the idea of destroying esthetics and denying the value of human culture.
[8] "Three Small Poems to Lenin" were published in Berlin in 1925.

Dear Laylee,

I regret very much that you did not do that translation,[1] and I ascribe the failure to your pointless trepidation. I personally wanted to see your name shine again in our literary firmament. In one way or another, it is still not too late and, if only you decide to do so, the State Press will be happily receptive to your work.

And about that wretched telegram, believe me, Laylee Mechlimovna,[2] it was done without my knowledge; they had simply reviewed the contracts as a routine check, and sent telegrams to all those who had not met the deadline. That's all. Kevork[3] says that the telegram left a bad impression on you. Your feelings are justified. But on its part, the institution is also right, because you could have at least notified us that the work would be delayed, and we could have extended the deadline. But let's leave this aside, let's forget it, and let me be permitted to dream that you will, one beautiful day, shine again on our literary horizon, and no longer conceal your talents, as you have been doing until now.

Accept my heart-felt greetings, dear Laylee; stay healthy and be bright of heart.

I shall be coming to Moscow,[4] but exactly when I do not know. But I'll definitely come. And then we can talk about everything with affection and without rancor.

Yours,

E. Charents

Erevan, October 29, 1933

[1] Reference is to an incident recalled by Laylee's husband, according to which Laylee had received an advance for a translation of Lermontov. The work was not submitted because Laylee became ill and couldn't work on it, upon which Charents had wired her to return the advance. When told of the circumstances, Charents apologized, explaining that the wire was a routine procedure, and not intended to hurt his friend.
[2] Charents invokes the well-known oriental legend, "Laylee and Mechnoon."
[3] Laylee's husband, Kevork Der Mekertichian.
[4] Charents went to Moscow in the summer of 1934 to participate in the first conference of Soviet writers.

(Telegram to Garen Mikaelian)
Please give Mikoyan a copy of my book without delay. I await your reply by telegram.

Charents

Erevan, 1934[1]

[1] The date of January 12 is inscribed on the telegram in Mikaelian's handwriting. On November 14, 1933, the secretariat of the central committee of the Armenian Communist Party decided against publishing Charents' *Book of the Road*, and relieved Charents of his duties as artistic director of the State Press. In December 1933 Charents was reinstated. Only a few copies of the 1933 edition of *Book of the Road* had been saved, one of which Charents had sent to G. Mikaelian to be given to Anastas I. Mikoyan. The book was published in 1934 without the play, "Achilles or Pierrot?", and other pieces, which were replaced by new work.

Dajad Khachvankian (1896-1940): Painter, and at the time chief designer for the State Press.

Dear Dajad,

I beg you to oversee the publication of Khachig Tashdents' book[1] personally, and see that it is printed tastefully, from the title, and the type, to the margins, so that everything is properly in its place. Khachig says that you have designed the book, and it remains for you to supervise the production.

The question of the cover remains. If what Shavarsh[2] has

prepared is unsatisfactory, let him design a new one. Give him some guidance. It will be better if it is in two colors and printed with an illustration. To avoid complicating this further, Chopour,[3] I think, will forego the jacket. You must resolve it by having a beautiful two-color cover designed; and if an engraving is necessary, Chopour can hardly object if a handsome exterior for the book results.

I fully hope that you will do whatever is possible to save Khachig's book from an unattractive exterior appearance.

Charents

Erevan, 1934

---

[1] *Songs of Spring*, a book of poems by Khachig Tashdents (1910-1974), published in 1934. It was dedicated to Charents on his 20th anniversary as a writer.
[2] The painter Shavarsh Hovannissian (1908-1980).
[3] Edward Chopourian (?-1938), director of the State Press.

Alexander Katov (b. 1899): Russian poet.

My esteemed Katov,

I received your letter and the translations.[1] I liked the translations of the rubayats[2] most especially, but I had some trouble understanding why you think the rest cannot be translated. In any event, that must remain your decision, and your personal concern. I have one request, however, a most urgent one. I want very much for all the rubayats to be translated for the volume of my work to be published by the Transcaucasian State Press. And if you cannot do it, can you recommend someone I can give them to, who will be able to translate them with sufficient understanding of their creative character? Should we approach Kuzmin,[3] or perhaps Shervinsky,[4] who is translating Virgil for "Academia?" Please give this some thought, keeping Folian[5] and me informed; also forward the literal translations of the rubayats, to facilitate the final renditions.

There is this question as well: I don't know what literal translations you have received from Folian. So I must ask you to return to Folian all those that have not been used, so that he may give them to someone else for translation. I urge you to do this without delay.

Now to your request. It is difficult for me to send you new literal translations; all I can do is advise you what to take from my most recent books. From *The Epic Dawn,* you might consider the following:

1. "To the Dashnagtsagans"
2. "Letter to A. Bakounts"
3. "Funeral March" (to Lenin)
4. "October 25-26, 1917"

The last can be titled "The First Day of October." (It is written in four-foot iambs, in the style of "The Bronze Horseman").[6] Try it, perhaps it will work. Chichikov[7] tried it once, but the result was very flat; he had demeaned both the style and content. I hope it will not be that way with you.

If these do not work out, or come to 400 to 500 lines, try selections from my last book (*Book of the Road*). I think you have a copy. I suggest the following:

1. "Seven Thoughts for the Builders of Cities"
2. "Seven Thoughts for the Poets of the Future"
3. "Ode to the Courageous Traveler"
4. "Ode to Nature"

Here is a complete plan for you.

I ask only that you let me see the translations. It will make me happy if you keep me informed about the progress of the work. I am prepared to help in whatever way possible.

Heart-felt greetings.

I await your answer.

> *Yours,*
> *Eghishe Charents*

Erevan, February 2, 1934

[1] Katov's letters to Charents and the translations have not survived.
[2] Katov had translated only nine of Charents' rubayats written in 1926; they were included in a volume of Armenian poems published in Moscow in 1934.
[3] The Russian poet, M. Kuzmin, did translate the 1926 rubayats, which were issued in Moscow in 1956.
[4] The Russian poet, S. Shervinsky, translated Charents' distiches, which were included in the 1956 volume.
[5] P. Folian was director of the Transcaucasian State Press in 1934.
[6] By Alexander Pushkin.
[7] Probably the Russian poet-translator, A. Chichikov, in whose 1933 volume from various Soviet nations, there was only one Armenian poem (by Ardashes Der Mardirossian); he was planning a second volume of such translations, but it never materialized.

My most esteemed Katov,

It was with the greatest satisfaction that I read your translations of my poems,[1] and I must tell you of my unqualified admiration of many of them. They are virtually equal to the originals. You have amazingly grasped and rendered in translation not only the literal meaning of the poems, line by line, but also (far more importantly) the actual style and spirit of the work, for which I am immensely thankful, with the gratitude both of a friend and a poet.

I particularly like:

1. "The Seven Thoughts"
2. "Childhood"
3. The first, third and fourth rubayats, most especially the first, which sounds just like the original. The rest seem a trifle ponderous, perhaps because of the very structure of those works. Aside from that, the principal requisite of the rubayats (from the standpoint of form) is for the rhymes, especially in the fourth and concluding line, to be particularly effective, otherwise they will be lost in the repetitions, and the quatrain will leave an inconclusive, blurred impression.

4. All the fragments of "Ars Poetica" are unquestionably good.

Frankly I did not like "To the Dashnagtsagans" and

"Meeting," perhaps because they have been translated without rhymes . . . Aside from Blok's fabulous work, I don't know of any Russian free verse which has profoundly impressed me. How then could ordinary mortals like us, driven by agitated desire, have any hope of succeeding? So, if you cannot shape them into rhymed iambs, give them to some other writer, especially "Meeting." I wanted "Dashnagtsagans" included for understandable reasons, but if it does not succeed, it is better to omit it than to print an inflated work of little real value.

Dear Katov, I liked your translations so much that I would rather not deal with any other translators for my work. Besides the Transcaucasian State Press, I have an agreement from "Soviet Literature"[2] for a collection of my poems. Would you assume the task of translating an additional 1,000 to 1,500 lines for that volume? If you agree, I will send you the literal, line-by-line versions of the poems, which, it is my hope, you will render in brilliant fashion.

I am curious to know if you have read any of your translations of my work to Russian poets? Do they fulfill themselves in Russian? They don't sound blurry or flat, do they? This worries me very much. Poetry, after all, is a very whimsical and deceptive thing. If it sounds profound and original in one language, that is not in itself an assurance that, when translated into another language, it will make the same impression. This torments me sometimes. Perhaps all my poems together are not worth a single wooden kopeck, and it may be presumptuous to offer them to such a sophisticated audience whose own poets include Pushkin, Blok, Mayakovsky, Pasternak. Is it appropriate for me to aspire to such a summit? Even the thought is terrifying; that so great a literature as the Russian, from which all kinds of Zharovs and Utkins emerge, cannot serve as hope and justification for a more or less serious man for whom poetry has not yet ceased to be a high rapture. Write to me, Comrade Katov, sincerely and without formality of any kind. Even the most devastating judgment will not hurt my feelings. For me it is better to know the truth right from the start, rather than be beguiled by false dreams. (Although I swear by poetry, I do not have large pretensions. I understand very well that a poet does not have to be renowned outside his own national literature. Are there so few, like us, among the Poles and Serbians, whose names we do not know?) This is the sort of thing that troubles me. What is it that can generate greater interest among you? Perhaps work of a philosophical nature, or with local color, or with contemporary revolutionary themes? In theme and genre, my writings have considerable breadth and variety, but a determination is difficult for me. My first concern is that I should differ in some way from the Soviet poets of today (from the standpoint of originality, individuality, depth); if this cannot be achieved, there is no point in insinuating myself into their midst. How sorry I am that you left so soon;[3] otherwise I might have been able to acquaint you with all my "creativity." (In our Union they have so debased the meaning of that word, one is ashamed to write it without quotes.) But you left. What can one do? One can only attempt to clarify everything through correspondence.

My dear Katov, I will await your answers to my questions; I would be very pleased, in fact, if we could correspond regularly, not only about such practical matters, but about poetry in general, and literature. But I fear that you are very busy. I have not received an answer to my first long letter. I think I told you about talking to Shervinsky about the complete translation of my rubayats (if it proved impossible for you to do them), and certain other things. Was the letter perhaps lost? It is possible that you responded, and that your letter never reached me.

Finally, about your own poems. I would gladly translate them into Armenian,[4] but I make this suggestion with some hesitation, fearing that you might interpret it as some sort of "bribe" on my part, with the ulterior motive of gaining your favor. I vow that it is not the case. And for a Russian poet, it is not so great an honor to be translated into a language which barely a million people can understand. With this I conclude my letter, hoping for a similarly long one from you.

Heart-felt greetings.

With sincere respects,
Eghishe Charents

Erevan, April 7, 1934

[1] All poems referred to in this letter were included by Katov in the volume, *Armenian Poets,* published in Moscow in 1934.
[2] The Soviet Literature State Press did not publish the volume Charents refers to.
[3] Katov visited Erevan for 10 days on November 23, 1933, with a group of Russian writers. It was at that time that he met Charents.
[4] As far as is known, Charents did not translate any of Katov's poems.

(To the Secretariat of the Armenian Writer's Union)[1]

I affirm that as of today I am resigning from the Writers' Union, wishing to devote my abilities (if such exist) to other areas of Soviet art such as the cinema, theater, opera or advertising. If I am unable to secure a minimum living in any of these careers as well, then I can apply to some factory, or find employment as a laborer.

Please accept this resignation without reading into it any ulterior motives, or political implications. I am not so idiotic as to protest against objective realities. As is evident, the writer of a small country cannot survive solely by his literary work. After a writing career of twenty-five years, I am convinced that it is impossible to maintain an average livelihood through literature. My collected works have been out of print for three years, in spite of demands for it from all sides. But the State Press refuses to issue a new edition, citing as justification the shortage of paper, and more urgent priorities. And I myself concur with the decision of the State Press. What then is there to do? To live only on translation and editorial work, after

creative endeavors of twenty-five years? I may agree. But . . .
the trouble is that even this kind of work is regarded as a great
benefaction that must be dispensed accordingly among all the
writers; with a limited amount available to each. It is far from
my intention to protest against all this. In constricted cir-
cumstances it is not possible to have "large" pretensions. And
what are those "large" pretensions? A monthly income of
2,000 rubles for which I am prepared to work fifteen hours
a day. But where can the State Press find enough such editorial
and other literary work?

I have not served art for twenty-five years to be left unable
at the end—even with ordinary literary chores—to secure a
minimum livelihood for myself and my family.

And what about the tax? I, who cannot even support my
family with literary and editorial chores, am obliged to pay
an income tax of 300 rubles a month because, unfortunately,
my book was published last year for which I was paid 10,000.
As if I kept that money in my pocket so that I could pay 300
rubles a month in income tax this year . . .

I repeat, I blame no one, least of all the Soviet apparatus.
It appears one must reconcile oneself with the natural reality
that the writer of a small nation cannot live by literature. It
remains then that he acquire another trade, and live by that.

Of all the Armenian writers (past and present), I am the
last to be accused of creative indolence. No other Armenian
poet has written as much as I have. To what avail? I certainly
can't produce a book of poems a day, and so support myself
with that. What would the quality of such work be, in the first
place? But even if I did, who is there to publish and pay for it?

I ask again that no political inferences be drawn from this
letter; and that from this day my name be removed from the
roll of writers. Perhaps I can be more useful in other realms
of Soviet culture and, at the same time, not be constrained
to beg for work and income.

E. Charents

Erevan, March 8, 1935

[1] The Secretariat of the Soviet Armenian Writers' Union considered Charents' statement in its session of March 13, 1935, judged it a "political document," and expelled Charents from the Union. In its June 6 session, a new application by Charents to be readmitted to the Union was considered and approved, following Charents' acknowledgment of his errors and promise to correct them. The signatories of this decision were Stepan Zorian, Terenig Temirjian, Axel Bakounts, and Trastamad Simonian.

Charents' statement was a direct reaction to some of the political and social aberrations of the 1930s, as well as the unfair attitude of the Writers' Union toward the poet. He was hounded and viciously attacked by a variety of enemies, especially after the publication of his *The Book of the Road.* Charents had expressed his deep dissatisfaction with the Union in a number of letters and poems written at the time.

K. Beiboutov (b. 1904): A journalist and an editor at the Transcaucasian State Press.

Comrade Beiboutov,

I received your letter some time ago but, as is my habit, I was waiting for an opportunity to send my reply. Comrade Bazhbeouk-Melikov will deliver this letter to you. As to Petrenko,[1] the translation, that is, I think it is marvelous. You can include it in the book. If you have any other literal, line-by-line translations, you can give them to him. The rest is up to you. When all the material for the book is ready, send the complete manuscript to me, so that I may put it into final form and authorize publication. Otherwise I could not consider the book mine. I have cautioned the Transcaucasian State Press many times about that, and I hope the book will not be submitted unless that basic condition is met.

Petrenko is an excellent translator, and I wish he could translate as many of my poems as possible. I would be grateful if you worked in this direction. Give him the ones Serebrovsky translated. I won't allow Serebrovsky's to be included in my book. When there is Petrenko, it is idiotic to accept Serebrovsky. That's all.

With warm greetings,
Charents

Erevan, 1935

[1] Bandelei Petrenko, a young poet, was to translate Charents' work, but he died prematurely. Bazhbeouk-Melikov is the painter H. Barzhbeouk-Melikian (1891-1966) whom Charents came to know well in the spring of 1935. The translator Charents refers to is Serebrianov, not Serebrovsky.

Boris Pasternak (1890-1960): Nobel prize-wining Russian poet and novelist.

Comrade Pasternak,

Please forgive me for the condition of the manuscript.[1] Comrade Nemchinov[2] rushed me so much that I could not have it copied or typed. Nevertheless I believe it is legible, surely enough to make a judgment of the contents possible. But for the shoddy appearance, I humbly beg your pardon.

1935

[1] The original is not complete and Charents' signature is missing; the page probably split at the fold. Charents couldn't have signed the letter. According to Beiboutov, this note was not delivered to Pasternak; the literal translations were given without the note. Pasternak translated only "The Curly-Haired Boy" which appeared in Pravda in November 7, 1935.
[2] Nemchinov was a contributor at the Transcaucasian State Press.

Sarkis Meliksetian (1899-1980): Deputy director of the Armenian Film Studio in 1935.

Dear Melikset,

I am in dire financial need. If you can, send me at least 300 rubles today, even if on account for the lyrics of "Alakiaz,"[1] or for whatever else. If it is not possible today, then surely no later than tomorrow. Please send word to my apartment.[2]

Charents

1935, Erevan

[1] The scenario for "Alakiaz" was by A. Bakounts and E. Grebner. The film was made in 1935-36. Charents also wrote the lyrics for "Bebo," the lead song of which, "The Net in My Hand," was put to music by Aram Khatchaturian, and proved very popular at the time.

[2] Charents' apartment in July 1935 was No. 6, Sundukian Street, now No. 45, Lenin Avenue.

Garen [Mikaelian],

I am so furious with you and—can you believe it?—a little with myself as well, that it is impossible to describe. I know you are angry too, but . . . who is to blame? We are, and only we, you and I, and everybody like us, that is, those Armenian intellectuals who are historically supposed to be the *bridge* between our past and present; but it appears that the bridge is shaky, has lost its identity, is pitiful and without purpose. Whatever. I have even dared to write about this in the poem dedicated to our 15th anniversary,[1] in which the poverty of the spirit of the Armenian people is represented as the most menacing evil to overcome. Those who are able to understand, understood.

But let's get to the main problem.

Garen!

Why is our attitude so poor? The reality was just the opposite, but it was precisely the opposite that came fatefully to pass.

Am I to blame or you? Let's leave that to God. But the relevant facts are these.

Arriving in Erevan,[2] I went to Aghassi[3] at the first appropriate occasion, and spoke to him in detail. He agreed to all my proposals, to all without exception.

As the concrete, practical conclusion to two immediate points, he personally recommended the following to me:

1. To wire you to go to Erevan, with your materials, so he can put the entire work in final form.

2. As to inviting Russian writers to take part in the 15th anniversary celebrations, he decided to wire the Cultural

House himself, and have the Cultural House issue the invitations in the name of the Government. We prepared the list of writers. You are mistaken to believe that Antokolsky wasn't among them. His was the first name on our list. As far as you were concerned, there was no question that your coming was in any way connected with invitations to other people. Even you yourself did not relate the two things; there was never any discussion about that between us. I decided to tell you as much about it as might generally interest you. Didn't you expect that they would invite you as a delegate to participate in the festivities? You did not raise such a question, nor was there any reason to raise it. All subsequent misunderstandings, yes, unfortunate misunderstandings, spring from this.

I wired you on Aghassi's official direction. (I am attaching the text of my telegram, word for word, to show you your mistake, and all the undesirable consequences stemming from it.)

The words might be a bit different (I don't have the original to copy from), but the meaning is accurate, word for word. What is essential here is your obligation to understand that your coming has no relation to the invitation extended to the Russian writers. As far as I know, you yourself saw none. No such problem existed. It was for that reason that I wrote at the beginning of my telegram that you leave for Erevan with the materials of the anthology, and only afterward informed you about inviting the writers, and that you would receive information about that (not about *your* coming). The information you were to receive (according to my telegram) concerned only the Russian writers, about which I apprised you as a matter of interest. Was it possible to conclude from my telegram that you were to receive an official request to invite the writers or, especially in relation to that, to go to Erevan? Was my telegram so incomprehensible?

You must have understood that your coming had no relation to it. My only purpose in mentioning it was to keep you informed about the matter. You should have known also that I could not, without official sanction, wire you to go to Erevan with the materials of the anthology. So . . .

Your telegram had a terrible effect on me. It was obvious that you were expecting an official telegram, tying your trip to Erevan to the invitation of the Russian writers. How could I have explained the circumstances in a telegram? I prepared ten drafts, but I found it impossible to explain this in a telegram, especially since it would have been inappropriate to mention Aghassi's name. After writing so extensively in a letter, I doubt that the reasons for the misunderstanding are any clearer. What could possibly have been done in a short wire?

And for the present.

Garen! With the official authority of Aghassi Khanjian I invite you (I repeat, he himself asked me to write to you officially) to come to Erevan, bringing with you all the materials for the anthology. This proposal remains in effect, and Aghassi does not even imagine that you are dissatisfied with anything. With what? I myself cannot understand it; how could he? I could not include his name in the telegram; it would have been inappropriate. His impression is that it is you who wish to be so informed about the desirability of your visit. And neither he nor I could conceive that this procedure would be offensive to you. That is why your telegram, and especially your last letter, had an extremely depressing effect on me.

Of course I have not said anything to Aghassi about this, and he is convinced that he has done whatever is best for both you and me. What it is that has hurt you I do not know. If we had known that you wanted yourself to invite the writers, on behalf of the Armenian Government, it would have been possible to have done it that way. But no such question had arisen. So Aghassi decided to have the invitation issued through the Writers' Union, to exactly those people on the list that we, Aghassi and I, had prepared.

I regret that because of this misunderstanding you were not present at the festivities. Now officially . . .

By the official authority of Comrade Aghassi Khanjian,

First Secretary of the Armenian Communist Party, I ask you in his name to take the anthology materials to Erevan, to secure final approval for it.

If, in spite of this, you wish to be informed in some other manner, wire me, and I will tell him that you prefer direction officially from him or, perhaps, from Trastamad.[5] Please! But he will wonder, in that event, about the purpose of all this talk.

Let us finish with this.

My advice is—and you will understand the intent of this—go to Erevan, together with the material, and all of us—you, he, and I—will be content.

Although my telegram, incorrectly interpreted by you, may not be an official document, you can present it to Aghassi, as the official authority for your coming to Erevan. The rest depends on you.

Yours,
Charents

P.S.: Wire me if you need money for your travel. But it would be better if you could somehow manage it, and not link the issue to it. Everything will be arranged here, and I think you will have no occasion to be dissatisfied.

I await your telegram.

Charents

P.P.S.: Just before I delivered this letter to Antokolsky,[6] I learned that Aghassi is going to Moscow[7] for a month, so that by the time you receive my letter, or perhaps earlier, he may already be there. You can meet with him and decide what to do. But, in my opinion, it would be nice if you came here. Aren't there other questions besides those related to the anthology that can be resolved here? It should be unnecessary to repeat why I am sending my letter with someone rather than by post. The reason is that I was waiting for an opportunity to be able to write to you in detail; while you, with amazing insensitivity, ascribe the delay to my carelessness.

Heart-felt greetings to you and to all. There are many new and interesting things here, but it is not possible to write about them now.

Char

You can simply tell Aghassi that, besides taking care of the anthology, other literary matters make it desirable for you to be in Erevan, that your receiving the authority from him to go to Erevan represents moral "encouragement" for you, or some such thing. He will gladly agree. I write this so that he does not think that by resolving the matter of the anthology, the issue of your coming is also settled.

In a word, do what you think is appropriate; but never allow the "evil" influences of Trastamad and others to assume vast dimensions. "The devil is not as terryfying as he is made to appear."[8]

[1] Reference is to "Fifteen Years," the poem Charents read during the celebrations of the 15th anniversary of Soviet Armenia.

[2] Charents had gone to Moscow in June 1935, and returned to Erevan probably in the beginning of November.

[3] Aghassi Khanjian (1901-1936), First Secretary of the Armenian Communist Party in Erevan in 1935, was executed during the Stalinist purges.

[4] Reference is to an anthology of Armenian poetry in Russian, from early days to modern times. Charents was to prepare one section on medieval and folk poems.

[5] Trastamad Der Simonian (1895-1937), chairman of the executive committee of the Armenian Writers' Union, was executed during the Stalinist purges.

[6] P. Antokolsky (b. 1896), Russian poet, came to know Charents in 1935.

[7] Khanjian went to Moscow at the beginning of December 1935, probably to prepare for the reception of the Armenian delegation at the Kremlin.

[8] Russian proverb.

[The letter is not dated. It was, however, written during the visit of Russian writers to Erevan for the celebration of the 15th anniversary. They must have departed between December 4 and 6, 1935, at which time the letter could have been written.]

Arax (b. 1903): Writer and editor of "Hokdemperik" magazine, which also published children's stories; in this capacity she had the opportunity to meet young writers.

Dear Arax,

This comrade—it was a surprise to me—seems to have the talent and inclination to become a writer of children's stories. He read a few to me and I liked them. He will surely be able to write such stories, if he is shown some guidance. Please keep in touch with him; you can help him with advice, subject matter, and so on. In a word, much depends on you if we are to develop a new writer of children's stories.

Friendly greetings,
Charents

Erevan, December 14, 1935

Moscow: Mikaelian   *(Telegram)*

Inform Postupalsky[1] that I don't agree to giving the rubayats to Roumer. His translations of Khayyam are unacceptable from the viewpoint of form. If Kuzmin[2] refuses, ask that Spassky, Lozinsky[3] or someone else be approached.

Charents

The end of 1935 or beginning of 1936

[1] I. Postupalsky was editor of the Charents volume being published in Moscow.

[2] M. Kuzmin translated Charents' 1926 rubayats. Charents wanted him to translate those in *The Book of the Road,* but he did not. O. Roumer subsequently translated nine of these which appeared in "Literaturnaya Gazeta," May 1, 1936.

[3] Both S. Spassky and M. Lozinsky translated Armenian poems for the anthology. Lozinsky translated the epic *David of Sassoun,* Erzenkatsi and Sayat Nova; Spassky translated K. Aghtamartsi and Telkourantsi.

Dear Garen [Mikaelian],

I received your letter and, taking advantage of Martiros'[1] trip to Moscow, I am sending along, not an answer actually, but greetings and news about things of interest to us, even if briefly, leaving the rest for a future meeting. As you learned from my telegram, the question of Trastamad's introduction is settled, and it has also been decided to use the "Briussov-Tikhonov-Antokolsky[2] variation. I sent the wire on the suggestion of Aghassi—even though our previous attempt may have raised some question about your requiring an "official" paper. I wired anyway; I also asked Aghassi, if at all possible, to apprise you himself as well. He said he would. Whether he did or not, I do not know, but even if he didn't, you can confidently have my telegram serve as a formal document. I think you may have done just that.

There is a lot to write about, but it is difficult to write. Perhaps you have heard that I am going abroad to convalesce. Soon I will be in Moscow to depart for Paris,[3] and we will be able to talk in detail. Martiros can tell you a good deal, but he is in a hurry now, so I must finish my "letter," adding warm greetings and my desire to see you soon.

Stay well.

Yours,
Charents

Erevan, May 20, 1936

---

[1] Charents sent this letter with the painter Martiros Sarian who went to Moscow to attend the opening of the exhibition of his paintings on June 7, 1936.

[2] Reference is to the problem of writing the introduction to the *Anthology of Armenian Poetry*. Charents wanted N. Tikhonov and Antokolsky to write the section on Soviet Armenian poetry, and use the one written by Briussov for other periods. The project, however, did not materialize during the purges of 1936-37. The volume was eventually published in 1938, with S. Haroutiunian and V. Kirpotin as editors.

[3] Charents had planned to go to Paris to convalesce. But not only was he unable to go to Paris, he could not even travel to Moscow. He was in disgrace, and would soon be imprisoned.

Isabella,[1]

Give this to Avetik,[2] but in such a way that absolutely no one becomes aware of it. Tell him to destroy it after reading or, if he should want to keep it, to show or mention it to no one.

Greetings. How I miss you, and Bozhik,[3] and Adok.[4] Ah, it may be better not to write. God willing, we will see each other soon.

Be strong, dear one, even if they should throw you out on the street. We are not the only ones suffering; there are many. Many others, people like us. Only work to support yourself and the children; I ask only that from you. May God be your guardian since, my dearest, we have no one.

I kiss you all a million times and more.

Yours,
Charents

Prison, October 6, 1937

[Fifty-four days later, on November 29, 1937, Charents died in prison, in circumstances still shrouded in mystery.]

---

[1] His wife Isabella. Charents married Isabella Niazian in 1931. After his arrest, she too was arrested and exiled to Siberia. After she was freed, she returned to Erevan where she lived her last years.
[2] Reference is to a poem dedicated to Avetik Issahakian. It was written on September 27, 1937 in prison, and sent to his wife along with the letter.
[3] An affectionate name Charents gave his eldest daughter Arpenig (b. 1932). The word comes from the Russian for "good," and the Armenian for "bauble," thus meaning something like "sweet-bauble."
[4] Or Adochka, the diminutive with which he referred to his younger daughter, Anahid (b. 1935).

Erkir Nayiri

Charents began writing *Erkir Nayiri*, one of the finest novels in modern Armenian literature, in 1921, and completed it in 1924, when he was 27 years old. By that time he had established himself as an eminent author as well as poet. One may, as the critic Souren Aghababian has noted, discern some Russian influences in the novel: Gogol's *Dead Souls*, for example, or Beli's *Petersburg* and *Moscow* or Saltykov-Schchedrin's *The Story of a City*. But the most relevant influence is from Charents' own cultural past, Abovian's *Wound of Armenia*, and Raffi's novels. But even in the latter instances, one must keep in mind that Abovian depicted the widespread misery that parched the Armenian landscape and seared the Armenian psyche; and that Raffi, going a step further, boldly asserted that the people could no longer supinely submit to persecutions, and must defend what was theirs as simple human rights—the sanctity of life and home—and in the process rekindled the Armenian national spirit.

At first glance Charents' work may not appear to fall in the same mold as that of Abovian or Raffi. His is a scorching indictment of the cowardice and treachery evinced by the inhabitants of an Armenian—in Charents' term, Nayirian—city, which in this case happens to be Kars, Charents' birthplace. He chose the fall of Kars as a representation of the momentous events that engulfed Armenia, in the flood of which a country was lost, and a people subjected to massacre. He resorted to satire to cope with the magnitude of the tragedy; it probably was not possible for him to do otherwise. He had depicted the enormity of the genocide in a somber poem, "Danteesque Legend," some years before; but turned to satire to portray the events that erupted from the violence of World War I. One could reproach Charents for his nihilism and iconoclastic tendencies, but that would not be entirely fair. There can be no doubt that he loved his country; witness his poem, "I Love the Sun-Baked Taste of Armenian Words," written at about the same time; but he could not bring himself to excuse the stupidity and the cowardice that resulted in the destruction of Kars and, by extension, Armenia.

Charents says there are no heroes in his novel, that it isn't his

intention to create characters and to explore their individual ex-
periences. While the central figure of Mazooti Hamo appears to
contradict this contention, it may not be unreasonable to consider
Erkir Nayiri, the country itself, as the hero of the novel. Was it not
Erkir Nayiri that was finally victimized, sacrificed by the short-
sightedness of those who loved it and were expected to defend it?
The structure of the novel, the course of events, and the fears of
the people who undermine the city's defense might suggest such
a possibility.

The entire novel is written in the form of an extended mono-
logue by the author directed to the reader. True the people are there,
they exist and do whatever it is they have to do; but they emerge
through the narrative of Charents who seems constantly to be ad-
dressing the reader, never letting him stray or get distracted in any
way.

The first part was written in Moscow in the fall of 1921, and
published in the magazine, "Nork," the following year. It contains
a graphic description of the city, its landmarks, the main streets and
the shops that line them, the shopkeepers, the ordinary people play-
ing cards and backgammon, or attending to their businesses; the
schools, the children, the various relationships that exist between
the characters; the routine, the customs and the color of the city
and its people. An authentic, living image emerges because, as the
author himself says, he knows the city as he knows his own five
fingers.

The second part was completed in Moscow in 1922, and again
published in "Nork" the following year. The war has already broken
out, inspiring hopes—depending on the expediency of czarist
policies—for a liberated Nayiri, and a euphoric atmosphere, the
enlistment of volunteers, the arrival of the national hero, Andranik,
and the subsequent departure of the volunteers to Erkir Nayiri to
deliver it from the enemy.

The third and final section was finished in August 1924, and pub-
lished in "Nork" in 1925. In this climactic segment, Erkir Nayiri
is liberated, for a brief moment. But czarist rule is overthrown;

the new regime has no interest in the policies of the czar; and with the issuance of Lenin's famous order, "Return to your homes," soldiers desert in droves. The Armenian troops are not immune to the lure of this summons, and they crowd into the city already jammed with refugees from neighboring villages. The city falls in spite of its adequate defenses. And the novel ends with the collapse on April 17, 1918.

The characters are based on real people who lived in Kars. Hamazasp Nohradian, one of the city's leaders, is seen here as Mazooti Hamo; the police chief Nicol Hagopian (1917-1918) becomes Comrade Varodian. The people and history have been faithfully transposed to fiction; it was an experience Charents had lived through; it remained for him to recreate it with an artist's vision.

There is a special significance to Charents' choice of Nayiri as the title of the book. It is the name of ancient Armenia, dating to Urartian times. At the turn of the century there was some disposition among the Armenian intelligentsia to revive some ancient values, and the name Nayiri was resurrected, with all the mystical aura it evoked. But it did not last. Certainly Charents wanted to see a resurrected Armenia. Who did not? But those in leadership at the time proved incapable of achieving it. They were tested and they failed. It is the crumbling of will, the lack of stamina that inspired Charents' pessimism and sarcastic thrust, and not the idea of a free Nayiri. He may assert that Nayiri is a "cerebral grief, a sickness of the heart," at the conclusion of his novel. It may have been to that "cerebral grief, a sickness of heart" that he eventually fell victim, many years after the fall of his Kars, in the heart of Erkir Nayiri, Erevan. And his quote of Derian's poem

> *Erkir Nayiri, distant dream,*
> *You're sleeping gently like a queen.*
> *Is it for me to sing a lullaby*
> *And put you in a royal cemetery?*

in the second edition of the book proved ironic. It was Erkir Nayiri that put the poet "in a royal cemetery."

Preface

For a long, long time an incessant ache has stirred in me, penetrating my entire being, desperately seeking a way out. In the dark of night, or in the brilliant light of day, whether I am occupied with routine concerns, or even transported by the enchanting pleasures of wine or a woman, *it* still moves inside me, quietly, deep in my heart, stealthy as a thief.

Like a promise made years ago, or like an obligation left unfulfilled, it weighs pitilessly on my heart, eating at it insatiably.

Often it takes the form of an old friend, someone I met a long time ago, but lost track of, who emerges unexpectedly from the past, staring at me through the indistinct haze. He looks into my eyes, staring, wondering. "Don't you recognize me?" he asks. "Have you forgotten?" he says. And glides away, to be enveloped in the mist again, and lost.

It comes to me in thousands of different forms. I may be reading a newspaper, or perhaps on my way to the market to buy wood. The seller is an ordinary peasant who has brought his wood to the market. "What's the price, friend, of your wood?" I ask. This much or that much. And for a moment he looks at me curiously. And—imagine, if you can— suddenly, in that casual meeting, through the mists of an ordinary peasant's eyes, *it* rises towards me again, somehow seeking me out, asking: "Don't you recognize me? Have you forgotten?" And instead of buying the wood I had come for, I turn back home, grief jabbing pitilessly at my heart.

Sometimes I see it in my father Abgar Agha's shiny yellowed hair. A thousand years old, it issues from the hair and looks at me. In countless guises, it looms before me. It lives, unseen, in everything that is ours.

But who is it? What is it? That's what matters most. Perhaps you will be surprised, dear reader, if I say that I don't know either. I know it exists, that it has existed and is old, as my blood is old. It is there; I feel it, see it, touch it with my heart; but as soon as I want to grasp it, place it firmly before me, it is lost, it fades, vanishes, like smoke or an illusion.

In our daily life, in the gray routine of living, it grieves unseen in the dark; it summons—but to where? When at dusk the old church bell sounds gently, distinctly, from the decrepit belltower, it calls. Who hears it? And if anyone does, how much does he understand? How much have I, who have heard its call from childhood, understood? Then why does it inundate me, why does the yearning flood my being? Why does it call to me? Intimately. Endlessly. And why do I keep searching for it? Why must I find it, speak to it warmly with the heart, love it?

Forgive me, dear reader, if you do not find answers to these questions in this book. The answers are in your heart, your soul. And you must feel the urge to find them. Nothing else can help. Nothing else.

How many times have I asked myself, what finally is Nayiri? Perhaps this question will seem strange to you; but it is no less natural than the question, who in the last analysis are we Nayirtsis? What are we and where are we headed? What were we yesterday, and what shall we be tomorrow?

Every time such matters consume my heart, some other being, it would seem, rising like a ghost from the mists of my life, has wickedly asked: "Wasn't it possible to present Nayiri as it actually was, or merely in the Nayirtsi way of life? To touch that actuality—the Nayirian—touch it with the heart, picture it on this earth. Perhaps Nayirtsis lie, perhaps it does not exist. Perhaps it is only a memory, fiction, myth. Hallucination, a sickness of heart."

I leave it for you, yes, you, to find Nayiri. In this poem-like novel, numerous Nayirtsis will pass before your eyes—love whomever you like, in the heart and soul of whomever you wish, find *Erkir Nayiri*.

And if you do not find it, be understanding. I am not at fault. Perhaps it is true that Nayiri is a mirage, a fiction, a myth. Hallucination, a sickness of heart. But in its place there is a country today called *Hayasdan*, and in that ancient land many very ordinary people have lived in the past, and live today, with the ordinary traits of people everywhere. And nothing more. Not an *Erkir Nayiri*—only people who are living today in that corner of our world which is called *Hayasdan*, now a Soviet Socialist Republic, while before 1917 it was nothing but a backward appendage of the Russian Empire, and nothing more.

Nothing more.

What remains is the novel.

Moscow, October 1921   *E. Ch.*

The City and Its Inhabitants

"Here the Nayirian charms . . ."—*V. Derian*

That ancient Nayirian city in every respect resembled all Nayirian cities, old and new; it was small, uncrowded, decrepit, and dusty. We might describe them today as backward, provincial cities. When was the ancient Nayirian city built?[1] Only God Himself knows. But they say that the founders were old Nayirtsis. Perhaps broad-shouldered, strong-armed Chaldeans, or curly-haired Urartians. But the origins may be of little moment because, of the old city, whether Chaldean or Urartian, not even the site seems to be left. Instead of their clay, subterranean huts, one-, two-, even three-storied stone structures, houses and shops, rose in that small Nayirian city—as much like those old Urartian huts as your nose, dear reader, is to the Eiffel Tower. Some of those new houses and shops had even been crowned with red or green tin roofs, a sign of the twentieth century, new and distinctive. In the unvaried sea of low-lying houses and shops, those roofs attracted immediate attention, much as a European chapeau, complete with a feather, would in an Eastern village. And it is not for nothing that even to this day they speak with awe and esteem about the man who was the first to cover his house with a tin roof. He was referred to as General Alosh,[2] known and respected by everyone, a venerable Nayirtsi past eighty, whom the reader will have further occasion to meet.

The houses in that Nayirian city, as I said, were low, most of them one floor, with slate roofs, but in the tedious flatness of those structures, in the very center of the city, stood—can you imagine?—a huge five-story anomaly. Whenever he passed that building, the well-known teacher of the parochial school, Maroukeh Drastamadian, himself no less a wonder in that Nayirian city, would mutter to his companions, or to himself if he were alone: "We are one thing; the Europeans something else." He would look admiringly at the strange small square windows of the five-story building, and add: "We are much too backward." This is what Mr. Maroukeh thought, and of course he was right. He had graduated from the local school, and by some accident of fate had been to Berlin for two or three months. At least that is what he had everyone believe. He liked only the new and the ideal, and couldn't tolerate anything old. And he enjoyed, justifiably, the reputation of a European in that Nayirian city; everyone, young and old, save for Comrade Varodian, a teacher at another school, respected him.

But besides that five-story miracle, the city had a number of wonders of its own, in which Drastamadian regrettably had no interest. But whatever he chose to think, without them the city would have lost much, if not all, of its charm, in the eyes of the inhabitants. And rightly so. Is the fort[3] any less a miracle? Or the Bridge of Vartan? Or the Church of the Apostles?[4] What about the Sellan Stone[5] in the valley, or the Chapel of the Hermit?[6] Which one shall I cite? All of them are miracles, extraordinary, impossible marvels!

Let us begin with the fortress which sits, harsh, forbidding, like a stern oriental tyrant, on the western edge of the city, high on the rocky yellow hill. From its lofty throne, it peers down on the city. It might be a vast assemblage of stones, dropped casually from the sky, left clinging tenaciously to the hill. One massive stone may have fallen first, with others following, streaming down, one after the other, large and small, heavy and light, variously shaped, landing one on top of the other, or side by side. It is a miracle, not to be understood, only to be marvelled at. It is said that the Nayirtsi masters used eggwhite instead of dirt when they built the fortress, and that's what made it indestructible. Everyone knows the fortress is inaccessible, and only treachery, vile, despicable Nayirian treachery, can deliver the fortress to murderous invaders. Only fools can fail to be entranced by that fortress, and one of those fools, permit me to say, is Drastamadian. Let that haughty "European" tell us how that ancient city could have defended itself against even the first of its enemies, had it not been for the fortress? It is from there, from those impregnable walls that shells will rain down, if war should come. It is from there, from those rocky barricades that the iron fist will descend one day, taut and tenacious, the invincible will of the Nayirian nation, the same iron fist that will come down hard on the enemy's head. This is what the fortress means, to one who understands, of course. Why else are the homes in the city below quiet and comfortable, seemingly unworried and secure? And the Nayirtsi shopkeepers lounging in front of their shops, yawning lazily and carelessly, waiting for customers? And what could it matter that now in 1913, by some idiotic and accidental quirk, it is not the Nayirian, but an eagle-adorned, flag[7] that flutters on the highest tower of the fortress? The Nayirtsis may have built the fortress, but tragically it was now serving to protect those invaders both from us, the real masters of the fortress and the city, and from every other enemy. They will leave some day. And again from the unreachable towers of the fortress, like an irresistible force, the same Nayirian spirit, the will, the strength—a thousand years old—of the Nayirian world, will rise again.

These were the feelings of the real Nayirtsis who inhabited the city. And how could anyone, even a European like Drastamadian, counter such commitment?

From both sides of that huge stone crate of a fortress, the remnants of the original ramparts straggled down the hill toward the city, like massively humped camels. In ancient times, the caravans of stone camels, solidly built ramparts, stretched out endlessly and—descending from the fortress, crossing the river, and taking the entire city within itself—for years on end protected the inhabitants from enemy and evil. Now only the humps of those huge animals, as crooked as the barren hills, have remained here and there. Now only the wondrous vestiges are left, one here, stuck to the fortress wall, another there on the river bank, and still another, far off beyond the city. Each of them covered over with moss. Anyone unfamiliar with the past might wonder who carved these stones out of the hills, designed them so beautifully, and laid them over with moss. A massive section of that legendary rampart still stood in the middle of the river that passed through the city. They called it the Bridge of Vartan. It was the general belief that this must have been a bridge, and one that only General Vartan could have built, because for the naive Nayirtsi of the day all that is great, wondrous and triumphant, all that is Nayirian, is ascribed to Vartan Mamigonian, the last regal Nayirtsi, about whom every ordinary Nayirtsi knows not much more than this: that on the Thursday before Lent mass is celebrated in his memory in all Nayirian churches, that "Lretz Amber" is sung, that it is a feast day, the name day[8] of all Nayirtsis. That's not the reason, of course, that the Bridge of Vartan has become a fabulous symbol for Nayirtsis. They say—and with conviction—that any who drown in the river are pulled down and gathered into the turbulent vacant depths under the bridge. They are certain that the huge mass of stone rises over an abyss. Under it there is nothing at all, nothing. And over that emptiness, an ancient wonder of Nayiri, the bridge has risen, hanging there, massive

and unmoving, the Bridge of Vartan. And in those vast bot-
tomless abysses, in which even water hesitates to flow, water
beasts flourish, witches, buffaloes with human heads, a
monstrous water snake which is lord of the region, the
benevolent spirit of the Bridge, and two water nymphs. Is it
surprising then that no one dares swim near the Bridge? How
often have gentle and intelligent Nayirtsis, while passing the
Bridge of Vartan at night, suddenly felt forces tugging at them,
pulling them down toward the abysses of the Bridge, sum-
moning them, charming them, seeking to draw them in their
depths!

How often did the priest, Fr. Hoosig,[9] warn his flock from
the stone pulpit of the St. Kevork Church that in such cir-
cumstances a real Nayirtsi must invoke the memory of Var-
tan the Brave, and draw on the faith of his forefathers. He
must recall the sacred purpose for which Vartan fell on the
field of Avarayr, and must not falter. And if he does not falter,
the evil power that hangs over the bridge of Vartan as a legacy
of the enemy, will vanish into the wind. And the Bridge will
be transformed into an altar of faith. *For the faithful the Bridge
of Vartan becomes a pillar of resurrection,* Fr. Hoosig has fre-
quently intoned. But it happens that at the most critical times
Vartan's name seems to escape the intellectual grasp of the
confused Nayirtsi, leaving in its place a vacant expanse, a
dreadful uncertainty, which seems paradoxically to increase
the insidious lure of the Bridge of Vartan. Still I can't imagine
how dismal and uninteresting the Nayirian city would have
seemed to its inhabitants had the Bridge not existed at all. Ac-
tually, it was not the only point of interest in the ancient city.
If the people had been asked to surrender any one of their
marvels, it is not at all certain that they wouldn't have given
up the Bridge in favor of the Church of the Apostles. It must
be said that, despite their fervent attachment to the Bridge
of Vartan, the Church of the Apostles represented more to
the people, as their most meaningful and sacred symbol, the
jewel and wonder of the ancient city. Whatever the soul is

to the body, the brain, the eye, the heart in the being of man, the Church of the Apostles was the same for that Nayirian city. What Notre Dame is to the Parisians, the Church of the Apostles was to the people of that city.

Perched on the side of the hill, north of the fortress and below it, the Church had the look of a grey bird carved out of stone. Viewed from above, from the fortress, it resembled a bird, but from the front it was more like a squatting priest, an old priest cut out of rock and sitting serenely on the side of the hill, for centuries, and as long as the world existed, the limitless world of *Erkir Nayiri*. Above, at the peak of the dome, was the plain, twin-winged Nayirian cross. And sloping down, its peak protruding in a curious point, the dome sat on an imposing square stone box.

Such was the Church of the Apostles. A miracle, can't you see? It is so obvious.

Ordinary, simple, as though the Nayirian spirit had assumed a palpable form. It is without adornments, externally; but for those who can see, wondrous and vast.

Let me tell you what others have told me about the Church of the Apostles. Believe it if you wish, or laugh. Whatever you prefer. But I haven't told you why it is called the Church of the Apostles.

On the dome of the Church, the Nayirtsi master sculpted the faces of the twelve apostles, one by one, side by side, all twelve. Do you understand? He carved those marvelous faces into the stone. Now the faces dug out of the hard, dry Nayirian mountain stone look serenely down from the musty, moss-flecked facade of the dome. The attentive observer will note that the face of one of the apostles is rough and repulsive. There is no nose, and instead of eyes are two black and grotesque holes. It is the face of Judas, people will readily explain, to whom the Christian master has given the appearance of a monster. It sometimes seems as though the face of Judas is not on the dome at all. Though the Church is formally named for the twelve apostles, the people stubbornly refer to it

as the Eleven Apostles, and with good reason. They do not
include Judas. They don't want to include him. But even with
this rejection, the Church of the Apostles does not forfeit any
of its centuries-old charm. Its mission is one thing, its charm
another. And I can give you a sense of that in what I will relate
now, dear reader, which you should not regard as empty
gossip or a contrived fable. If by some chance you ever find
yourself in that city, ask about the Church of the Apostles,
and everyone will tell you the same thing, and perhaps even
more.

This is the story of what occurred.

A house half in ruins still stands about two or three hun-
dred paces from the Church, beside the road that leads to it.
The walls remain though the roof has collapsed, and the small
house is a pile of rubble, a doorless ruin. Only twenty or so
years earlier the house had both door and windows, and a
Nayirian refugee lived in its low damp rooms; he is known
to everyone now as Tato of Moosh.[10] His life was marked with
misfortune; he lost his family in a massacre that struck a dis-
tant Nayirian city. He escaped, took refuge here, destitute,
and by some turn in his luck, found habitation in that decrepit
hut near the Church. Tato of Moosh lived there for a few years,
aware of nothing around him. One day in the market he met
a friend from his native city. He had just come and told of
horrible things that had happened there. The same story over
and over: *Massacres, massacres, massacres.* Raped women, lost
children. And escape, exile, destitution. Tato of Moosh listened
and remembered his own, remembered his wife, his children.
Together they went to a tavern and began drinking—bitter
Nayirian *arak*, with the taste of blood. Then Tato began to
tell his friend about his city. They stumbled out of the tavern.
They saw the *fortress,* the Bridge of Vartan, the Church of the
Apostles. His friend said: "The day will come when the
Nayirian spirit will rise again, be resurrected from the mist.
Powerful, firm, the vengeance of iron will descend on the
enemy's head." With such thoughts on their minds, they finally

reached Tato's house, and lay down immediately to sleep. And
there at midnight, Tato thought he heard a sweet voice call-
ing to him. From below, from the basement, a familiar voice
was summoning him. He got up and called to his friend, come
on. He picked up his lamp and together they went below.
Damp, filled with stale air, horrible. For a moment they stood
still, confused; a sad, clear voice kept calling. They stared at
the floor; a heavy millstone seemed embedded there. It looked
to them like a door. Tato placed his foot on the millstone; it
moved. They bent down and raised the stone, and a dark
passage opened beyond it. Dark and damp, a wet draft blew
across their faces. Straining to see, they made out the stairs
ahead. They raised the lamp and went down. The stairs ended
at the head of a dark corridor—leading where? They went
along the corridor, walking, walking. The corridor widened.
And once again—stairs. They went up and suddenly emerged
. . . into the Church of the Apostles. The chancel, the altar,
and above, the curtain, a dark blue curtain with a golden cross
on it. And there the basin in which infants are baptized. They
didn't know what to make of it. They tried the doors, wanting
to get out. The doors were locked. Terrified they ran back.
They walked through the same corridors, walked a long time;
and then again the stairs. And suddenly, above them, below,
around them, on all sides, they heard the deafening clamor
of rushing waters. They ran up the stairs and got out. The
lamp was almost extinguished by the dampness and the wind.
Where were they? They had no idea. They could only sense
that they were standing on some high place, shuddering from
the dampness. Below them, the river, the swirling current,
the surge of water; above the sky. Dark, dank night. And sud-
denly Tato realized that they were on top of that very hump-
like remnant of the old fortress wall, in the middle of the river.
The Bridge. The Bridge of Vartan, as the people called it.
Beyond the waters, below, old women were singing. Or was
it the sound of the waters? And through the surging, fluid
darkness, a sinuous light glistened intermittently, as the snake,

the benevolent spirit of the Bridge, moved in and out. Then
the hoarse, terrifying tumult of water buffaloes emerging from
the foaming waters. They were sick with fear and disbelief.
Quickly they ran down, escaped through the corridors. Then
again, steps. So many of them, so many! They went up, up,
up, until they found themselves outside again. Around them
was the sky, mist pierced by stars. Below them the city. Sparse,
yellow fires flickered. Far, far in the distance, the sad, soft
rustle of the river could still be heard. And under their feet,
the fortress. The crate-like stone formations squatted imper-
turbably, ponderously. They were standing on the highest
tower of the fortress. A sharp, cold wind burst against them.
Nearby the fortress flag flapped feverishly. It was dark; other-
wise they would have seen the two-headed eagle, in ornamen-
tal gold on the yellow standard. It was night, it was dark, so
it couldn't be seen. The wind swirled furiously. They could
not stand it. Why were they there? What did they want?
Bewildered, terrified, they ran down the steps again, and into
the underground corridors, breathless and confused, and
drenched in sweat. Suddenly, without knowing how, they
stumbled into their basement and up into Tato's room, and
collapsed into a dead sleep, a bitter, dreamless, heavy sleep.
But they were cheerful and bright in the morning, anxious
to tell everybody what they had experienced; everybody was
amazed and confused. There were those who considered the
accidental discovery a mysterious omen, the augury of a new
awakening. It is near now, they were supposed to have said,
the moment of rebirth. And they warned Tato and his friend,
cautioning them strongly not to talk about it further.[11] Now,
twenty, twenty-five years after the remarkable incident,
everybody—even the children—knows about the corridors and
the stairs in the fortress, the Church, and the Bridge. But they
never talk about them. It is forbidden to talk about them. As
for Tato, when, because of his and his friend's carelessness,
the government learned about the secret of the Church, they
seized it, and exiled Tato and his friend to Siberia, to rot in the

damp dungeons there. This is what the Church of the Apostles came to represent. And more. Beyond those miracles, there were Nayirian kings buried[12] in the Church. And when the Church was occupied and the floor torn up, numberless, priceless treasures and artifacts were discovered. It's an old, dark history. Which part shall I recount? The Nayirian kings had been wise, clever, rich and proud. There are no such kings now. They had been wise, clever, rich and proud, but selfish and divisive too. Otherwise why would their kingdoms have vanished, and the land of Nayiri transformed into ruins? Where are the miracle-working Nayirtsis now, where is the thousand-year-old Nayiri? It does not exist. Nothing exists now. Even the ancient Nayirian city where the wondrous old miracles had taken place, once the seat of kings, a capital, an ancient center, even that city has, in the grip of foreigners, become a provincial backwater where corrupt functionaries caught in various abuses are exiled for punishment.[13]

Towards Nayiri

The days that followed brought misfortune, not only to that city, but to all Nayiri—desperate days that still managed to produce leaders both tragic and heroic. Nor could the fire of that sad time fail to resurrect the bright and sacred spirit of Nayiri.

I remember that historic day in all its details, as clearly as my meal this afternoon. It was a July Sunday in 1914, in that Nayirian city. At this very moment, as I begin to describe the events of that memorable day, the incidents and images come together before my eyes, rising, as the poet might say, from the dark cold ashes of the past. Clear, precise, as if it had all happened yesterday, or even an hour ago. Here is Mazooti Hamo, in front of the office of the city's public garden, standing on a green card table, delivering a speech. It is as though it were happening now. I hear his distinctive voice, his powerful delivery. The glittering eyes of Hamo Hampartsoomovich peer at me through the late night darkness of my room, and my heart begins to pound with remembered emotion, signalling its perplexity like the silver-coated tongue of an electric bell. And leaping ahead, my imagination becomes a pitiless executioner evoking the image of Mazooti Hamo hanging from the gallows like a wooden mannequin. "Poor Hamo," my heart murmurs. I am on the verge of tears; I put down my pen to give my heart a chance to recover, and permit me to resume my story.

The Nayirian city was enjoying a lazy, peaceful Sunday respite. The bell of the Church of the Apostles had sounded, but without urgency or insistence. Whoever wished to pray had gone to church, but most of the city dwellers were in the public garden, or sitting in front of the closed shops, exchanging news about themselves. Some had gathered in the cafes of Telephone Seto or Egor Arzoomanov. Others had met in the clubhouse of the public garden to play cards. Among them that day were Sergei Kasparich, the doctor; Osep Narimanov, the judge; Aram Antonich, the school principal. Mr. Maroukeh, Kindauer[14] Simon who liked the company of "important" people, the English-speaking businessman Haji Onnik Manookov Effendi, and a few others. They played "preference," "macao," "baccarat." They liked to play, and as a rule played quietly, with formality, breaking the silence occasionally only with such exclamations as "Pass," "28," "Dalia." But despite their complete immersion in the game, some, particularly Sergei Kasparich and Osep Narimanov, had a sense of uneasiness. They seemed to feel that "something" was in the wind, notwithstanding the pleasant July weather. They kept looking at the door and the window. Something seemed to be missing, something they had all become accustomed to, if the word "something" could be used to refer to a person, and an estimable one at that. General Alosh was absent. Without him there was no life in the clubhouse, especially since the second moving spirit, Mazooti Hamo, was also missing. Even before the game had begun, Osep Narimanov had asked about him; actually it was when he had entered the clubhouse that, as was his custom, Osep Narimanov joyfully exclaimed: "My deep respects to Aliosha Nikitich." But he received no response for the very good reason that Aliosha Nikitich was not there. He was surprised, and he began thinking of what reasons might have detained him. When he had left the clubhouse early that very morning, General Alosh had promised to be back at ten o'clock to finish the interrupted game. Also, lately the General had been looking with a calculating eye at Olga Vasilevna, the blond pumpkin. But Olga Vasilevna was his, his, Osep Narimanov's alone, and could not belong to anyone else. Let General Alosh be well aware of this. Hardly had these thoughts settled in Osep Narimanov's mind when Aram Antonich, about whose wife his friend, the judge, seemed so concerned, burst in, and noticing that things were already under way, grabbed Osep Narimanov's arm from behind. He was still out of breath as he suggested a hand of "macao" or "preference." "My deepest respects," Osep Narimanov exclaimed happily. "How is Olga Vasilevna, Aram Antonich?" It only occurred to him then that he had not seen Olga for three days. He had tried at six o'clock in the evening the day before when, as was his custom, he went to "visit" her (Aram Antonich was usually in school at that hour); but the maid explained that Olga Vasilevna had left instructions to admit no one. Remembering this incident, Osep Narimanov's eyes had already begun to darken, and he wanted to blot out Aram Antonich from his view when the words, "Warm greetings from Olga Vasilevna," issued from his smiling lips. Then leaning toward Narimanov's ear, he went on in a whisper: "Mamasha [Axiona Manookovna, the midwife] swore yesterday that this time definitely, most definitely, it will be a boy." Osep Narimanov felt a heavy stone lifted from his heart. His long years of intimacy with Olga had not apparently been unavailing. He was elated by the prospect, acknowledging his joy by shaking the hand of Aram Antonich. "I have the honor to be the godfather of Kolechk. Do you understand, Aram Antonich? It must be so." The matter seemingly settled, they sat to play. "And where is Aliosha Nikitich?" Aram Antonich asked a moment later, as he began to deal the cards. But everyone was already preoccupied with the game, so nobody, in spite of the awareness of the General's absence, answered. Only the Doctor Sergei Kasparich stared again at the window, thinking again that "something" was up; but he realized that his uneasiness was not caused by that, said nothing and continued to play.

It was about noon. General Alosh and Hamo Hampartsoomovich, Mazooti Hamo, surged into the clubhouse like a tidal wave, pounding the tables and sweeping the cards to the floor. The players were stunned into silence. In spite of his being the big loser and so most likely to be resentful, Kindauer Simon was as perplexed as the others, his first thought being that they must be drunk. He flung his cards in the air as he got to his feet, shouting unintelligibly, "Hoorah! Hoorah! Hoorah!"

"What is this, have you gone mad?" the doctor shouted angrily, thumping the table for emphasis. "What has happened?"

The others had not yet been able to collect themselves when Hamo Hampartsoomovich raised his hand and signaled for silence.

"War," Hamo Hampartsoomovich announced in a muted voice.

Astonishment followed by silence.

General Alosh was also preparing to say something. He raised his hand, but affected by the solemnity around him, could not speak. Aram Antonich's smile remained fixed on General Alosh's raised hand. An idiotic smile was frozen on Kindauer Simon's face. Sergei Kasparich moved his hand to his lips almost mechanically, as he often did when seeing a patient, and coughed his dry, official cough. Then General Alosh and Mazooti Hamo related what had happened, as they knew it. At seven or eight o'clock in the morning, when Hamo Hampartsoomovich was still asleep, and aware of nothing, he was awakened by a summons from the provincial governor who wanted to see him immediately on an urgent matter. He had also asked that Aliosha Nikitich accompany him. Mazooti Hamo quickly dressed and rushed to the General's home, and together they set out for the provincial governor's residence. The latter received them with great courtesy, despite the unusual hour. "By the will of God," he told them, "and the august Emperor, Russia has been forced to declare war . . . that is, the villainous German Emperor Wilhelm II has declared war on Russia. It is necessary to organize demonstrations immediately," the governor went on, "and make the people understand the significance of this."

Hamo Hampartsoomovich's words exploded like bursts of thunder. They all stopped playing cards and, led by Aliosha Nikitich, went out of the clubhouse. "Gentlemen, we must begin," Hamo Hampartsoomovich told them at the door. "Begin what?" Kindauer Simon asked, upset. It seemed to him that the beginning they were talking about was the war. "You'll see in a moment," Hamo Hampartsoomovich replied mysteriously and reentered the clubhouse, Kindauer Simon following him. They emerged once again, holding a large picture of the Emperor; behind them was the club caretaker who set up a green card table. General Alosh and Osep Narimanov held the Emperor's picture. Mazooti Hamo got up on the table, with the people closing in around him. "Gentlemen!" Mazooti Hamo raised his hand, and with that one gesture seemed to turn everyone to stone. It was a miracle performed by a master prestigitator.

Perched on the pedestal of the card table, Hamo Hampartsoomovich looked down from that eminence and began talking about the war. He cursed, his eyes projecting sparks, he lashed at the German Emperor, Wilhelm II. The small grocer, Kolopotian, standing in the crowd, pictured the evil Wilhelm as Mazooti Hamo's sworn enemy, accountable directly to him; while to the barber Vassil, loitering on the fringes, the Emperor emerged as a blood-thirsty beast. Mazooti Hamo did not forget to relay the most important part of what the governor had told him, that our omnipotent king-emperor had sent numerous telegrams to Wilhelm, proposing to resolve their differences peacefully, but it was of no use. Mazooti Hamo concluded by exhorting everyone to rally behind the fatherland, in this difficult hour, sacrifice willingly for the welfare and safety of their country. "Long live our king-emperor, and our glorious army; may the despicable Wilhelm II be destroyed! Hoorah!" Mazooti Hamo was astonished when he stopped; there was only silence. It was not, however, because the people were disinterested or unmoved. No. They simply did not know, had not yet learned, how to respond to such occasions. Then General Alosh, with his considerable prestige, came to the rescue. With an agility surprising in a heavy old man, he jumped up onto the table and stood beside Mazooti Hamo. "Hoorah!" he shouted, waving his hat. A raucous echo issued from Sergei Kasparich, Osep Narimanov, and Kindauer Simon. And immediately from one end to the other, the public garden resounded with the roar, so loud that even Mr. Maroukeh, who had already parted from his card-game companions and was milling around in the crowd, seemed momentarily confused, and on the verge of raising his hat and joining in the excited response. But Mr. Maroukeh did no such thing. From the very first, he had determined his own particular position on the events that had transpired—but of that, more later.

The clamor of joyous exclamations soon gave way to the strains of martial music. The military band dispatched by the governor was playing "Pozhe Tsaria."[15] The men responded by removing their hats. When the anthem ended, Osep Narimanov shouted: "Long live our dear Emperor Nikolai II. Hoorah!" From the top of the table, General Alosh and Mazooti

Hamo continued their exhortations. After a time, they got down and, led by these two venerable Nayirtsis, a procession of the townspeople emerged from the public garden and moved down the principal avenue towards the home of the provincial governor.

When the procession, to the accompaniment of the band, passed by the cafes of Telephone Seto and Egor Arzoomanov, the Nayirtsis who had gathered there to play cards, dominoes, or backgammon, were attracted by the commotion, and watched as the parade surged past them. "What is this mob after?" Enoch the coffin-maker wondered out loud, the queen of spades still in his hand. "It looks like they will be raising the price of bread again," was Telephone Seto's curt rejoinder as he went back into the cafe, shaking his head. "I can never understand why they make all this fuss," he muttered once inside, to no one in particular. He neither expected nor got an answer, since everybody was still outside watching the procession. "Let them blow their horns as much as they want to; the price of bread will go up anyway," he repeated when his customers came back to resume their games. "I wonder what it could be," Kor Aroot mused, and the Nayirtsis shook their heads thoughtfully. But a few, like Mr. Abomarche, the French grocer, Daniel the Catholic, and others, observing that the parade was led by such prominent Nayirtsis as General Alosh and Mazooti Hamo, followed the procession. Quickly it became obvious to all that they were on their way to the governor to declare their patriotism and loyalty, something, it seemed to Mr. Abomarche, altogether most appropriate and desirable. "I wonder up to what age they will call up the men?" Daniel the Catholic mused. "Who knows?" Mr. Abomarche reasoned. "It depends on the circumstances." They kept walking, silenced by their own thoughts, their eyes fixed on their own shoes.

It was a warm Sunday, the golden hue of the sun everywhere. The cloudless sky lay over the city like an inverted blue tray. The band kept playing and the people in their colorful Sunday clothes followed it. And for the young ones clustered near the band, it all seemed like a holiday they enjoyed without understanding. A ten-year-old, the son of Haji Onnik Manookov Effendi, whose mischievous nature was well known to all, was marching proudly beside the drummer, trying to make himself look like a soldier, keeping time out loud: "One-two! One-two! One-two!" At last the procession reached the governor's house. The band played "Pozhe Tsaria" again, and the governor came out onto the balcony. "Hoorah!" the crowd roared, led by General Alosh. Then silence, sudden and death-like. All eyes were on the balcony. The governor was thin and tall; from a distance he looked like a long slender cane, topped with an onion. For a moment or two he looked down on the crowd gathered below. His hand went to his mouth to suppress a cough perhaps. Then he started to speak in the dry clipped manner of the military. *War. Emperor. Wilhelm II. Duty. Service. Fatherland and throne. Long live. Down with. Hoorah!*

Again the crowd applauded; again the band played "Pozhe Tsaria"; and again Mazooti Hamo appeared. The faces of the townspeople gleamed with pride, Nayirtsi faces blossoming like unfolding roses. What would that Nayirian city have done, I wish someone would tell me, had it not been for Hamo Hampartsoomovich, the director of "Light,"[16] Mazooti Hamo. It would have been lost, it would have been trampled, it would have been buried in unending darkness. He was everywhere, in every difficult situation, he and only he could lift the wagon out of the mire. And now again. Mazooti Hamo vowed on behalf of the people that they were all ready to fight to the last drop of their blood, for country and for throne. Hamo Hampartsoomovich understood well what needed to be said and how. He had a serpent's wily tongue.

When Mazooti Hamo finished, the grateful governor expressed his thanks to the people, and told them it was best to go home and tend to their family needs. General Alosh, Hamo Hampartsoomovich, Osep Narimanov and the doctor were invited for dinner. The rest dispersed, some going home, some back to the cafes, and still others to the public garden where they would pass the rest of the day.

It was with such ceremony and excitement that the Nayirian city welcomed the bloody guest, world war.

It was about eleven o'clock in the morning when the volunteer troop the people were dreaming about finally entered the city in brisk military formation. But before its arrival, anxious Nayirtsis, led by Mazooti Hamo and Comrade Varodian had gone to the train station to welcome the men. Almost everybody was there, from General Alosh to Enoch the coffin-maker. Enoch and Kor Aroot, it might be said, were there as a matter of course, and not out of any particular desire; but Kindaur Simon, Mr. Abomarche, the Haji, the barber Vassil, and a lot of others, had interrupted their work to participate in the welcome. Nor am I referring to the craftsmen or the enlistees who had come to see the troop. The most indifferent were the people on Loris Melikian street, the grocer's district, which had virtually no representation at all at the station that day. The shopkeepers did not consider it necessary to leave their work. It wouldn't have made any difference; the volunteers would have had to pass their street in any event, and they would be able to welcome the heroes in front of their own shops. On the other hand, all the intelligentsia were in the station, the teachers, the Nayirtsi officers, the students, many of the civic functionaries. Present also were large numbers of students who had sacrificed their classes that day for the sake of the fatherland; some of them were already thinking of sacrificing not only their classes, but also their lives for that most sacred cause.

Five minutes before the train pulled in, Hamo Hampartsoomovich, Comrade Varodian, the doctor, Osep Narimanov, General Alosh, and Kindauer Simon were already on the platform. They were the official reception committee. At their side was the military band which had been instructed by Comrade

Varodian to play the Nayirian anthem, "Our Fatherland."
Everything was considered in readiness to receive the
volunteer troop with appropriate ceremony and enthusiasm.
And behind the leaders solid rows of townspeople had formed,
all watching the tracks, impatient for the arrival of the train.
"It's late," General Alosh, already worried, said to Mazooti
Hamo, as if the latter were responsible for the delay. But at
that very moment the train whistle signaled the good news
of their arrival; it was the signal too for everyone to begin
stirring, pushing each other and, instead of feeling content that
the train had finally arrived, to become even more impatient.
At a sign from Comrade Varodian, the band struck up the
Nayirian anthem as the train slowly pulled into the station.

It is difficult, dear reader, to describe with my inadequate
pen, the fervor which infused the Nayirtsis on that historic
occasion. Hardly had the first military caps been sighted when
the entire station shuddered with the roar of welcome. And
when the train and the leader of the group, the renowned
soldier,[17] came out of the car, Mazooti Hamo and Comrade
Varodian rushed toward him, their hats in their hands; and
the leader of the volunteers embraced them, first Mazooti
Hamo and then Comrade Varodian. Do you understand? Then
Comrade Varodian. This when even shaking the hand of the
famous leader was no more than a dream for Osep Narimanov
and General Alosh, to say nothing of Kindauer Simon. While
all these unbelievable things were happening, the repeated
explosions of "Hoorahs" echoed in the city. "They must have
arrived," Kolopotian said to a customer, and even his face
brightened with a happy Nayirian smile. The volunteers de-
trained and, on the orders of the commander, stood at atten-
tion in the station. And Mazooti Hamo, the irreplaceable
Mazooti Hamo, began his speech. "Welcome," he said, "you
have a special place in our hearts." And he went on to talk
about the meaning of that unforgettable day. "This historic
day shall have a place among our greatest national and church
holidays, and the future Nayiri will celebrate it as it does Var-

tanank, Christmas and Easter. A free and independent Nayiri will celebrate it on the other side of the frontier, where our suffering brothers are now waiting for deliverance. Go," he ended his speech, almost in tears. "Our beloved brothers are still suffering there in the claws of oppression, our native land still sweats blood from the yoke of the barbarian. Go! Brave, invincible champions of our unrelenting will. We will be thankful to you, as we are thankful today. Go! I believe in the future free and independent Nayiri." The crowd roared with approving "Hoorahs." Still tense with emotion, he approached the commander. "May I be permitted," he said, embracing the commander, "to kiss this forehead, dear countryman, which has never feared the enemy's bullet, which has faced it with contempt and, I am convinced, will continue to do so for a long, long time, until the day of victory."

The Nayirian anthem rang out again, resounding with the voice of freedom. In the eyes of many of them, even those of Enoch the coffin-maker and Kor Aroot, there were tears of joy. Then the commander, briefly, as befits a soldier, thanked his dear countrymen who were not niggling in their support and respect for their sacred task. "But," the commander said at the end, "if only one percent of that respect took the form of deeds, of practical help, I too, like Mr. Hamazasp, would not doubt for a minute that the day is not far off when the land of Nayiri shall be delivered."

The commander concluded with these strong, pointed words and then, after the Nayirian anthem and the "hoorahs," he added, almost as an afterthought, "may the invincible sword of our king-emperor always be sharp, because only by his royal will shall the land of Nayiri be delivered." After these words, the band played "Pozhe Tsaria." The hats came off again, while the commander and Comrade Varodian, who for the past few days had been wearing a volunteer's uniform, saluted.

"Long live the king-emperor," Mazooti Hamo shouted, waving his hat, as though only now remembering the inexcusable omission during his speech. Then the music and "hoorahs" stopped, and it was all over. The commander, Mazooti Hamo, and Comrade Varodian got into the first car, the bodyguard, the doctor and General Alosh in the second, while Osep Narimanov and the others in the remaining cars, and they set out for the city, followed by the happy glances of the Nayirtsis.

An hour later, under the command of an aide, the volunteer group also entered the city, where it was again greeted with ardent enthusiasm.

The Land of Nayiri

It was on the day the "telegraph poles" were being erected that Mazooti Hamo returned unexpectedly to the city. Whatever areas could have been occupied were already occupied; more, the enemy, that *eternal invalid,* by some unbelievable miracle, had already penetrated the frontier, and had deployed his ragged troops some thirty miles from the city. Like frightened cattle, the Nayiri soldiers had fled before the enemy, and poured into the city. No deserters were left dangling from ropes. Was it possible to hang an entire army from three telegraph poles? It is difficult to describe what the city had become. Just imagine getting up some morning and, as you reach for your clothes, finding that by some incomprehensible sorcery all the stitches had become unravelled. Parts of your shirt fall away, piece by piece, the sleeves here, the collar there, the rest somewhere else. You try to pick up your trousers, and the same thing happens. And that's not all. A fire suddenly breaks out in your apartment. What are you to do? Run out? But there are people, women and children, outside. You can't run around naked in front of them, can you? Will you stay inside then? But the smoke is already beginning to choke you, and in less than a minute the red flames will begin brushing your body. It was just such a dilemma that confronted Mazooti Hamo when he returned from the "occupied areas." All the stitches of the city had been ripped away, the separated parts haphazardly dispersed, and the fire beginning its assault. The smoke was already suffocating the city, the red flames like a rear guard roaring impatiently behind. What was there for Mazooti Hamo to do? Flee? Stay? But how could he flee? Could a man's soul escape and leave his own body to be burned? Mazooti Hamo stayed. Not only did he stay, but he assumed complete command. He wanted to give himself completely in a final thrust to salvage the situation. But nothing could be saved. It was too late, much too late, and no one, not even with superhuman powers, could do anything about it.

How could Mazooti Hamo possibly do anything when, as we have said, all the stitches that held the city together had become undone, and not even the most ingenious "tailor" could repair the damage, and rejoin the parts that had not only been torn from each other, but had already begun to appear incompatible? During the absence of Hamo Hampartsoomovich, conditions in the city that were making its various elements fly apart were so severe, that it was no longer possible to relieve, let alone neutralize them. This is what Mazooti Hamo found when he returned to the city after only a month's absence. The first thing he did was hurry to the fort. No commander should be compelled to witness what he found there. The fort which Nayirian kings had built, and which had braved a thousand enemies and a thousand misfortunes, was in pitiful condition. The dreams, the expectations of centuries, emerged from the mists of the past, and stirred in Mazooti Hamo's embittered heart. Is this how Mazooti Hamo had foreseen this day? Is this how his brilliant mind had envisioned the Nayirian fort in those distant days rich with hope and anticipation when, no more than a director of "Light," he sat in the offices of the company? From here, from the stone ramparts of this fort, perhaps shells would have been fired one day, if that day ever came. From here perhaps, from these ancient parapets, the irresistible will of the Nayirian nation would burst forth, like an iron fist, against the enemy's head. The Nayirian spirit would soar from this impregnable height with the will and strength of a thousand years of the Nayirian world. And ancient Nayiri, a thousand years old, would come alive again, smiling ecstatically. This is what Mazooti Hamo had dreamed during those restless nights in the offices of "Light," waiting for this day. The day came. By some miracle, the armies withdrew from the Nayirian world, and suddenly the land of Nayiri assumed recognizable shape, suddenly it became a reality. And then? Terrified by the hordes of the *eternal invalid,* shocked by the shards of death splintered from their forces, the Nayirian armies thundered away like frightened cattle. Only the fort was left, this Nayirian fort which will be overrun by those hordes tomorrow. It will once again be compelled to lick their feet, and breathe the dust of their boots. What happened to the strength, the will of the ancient Nayirian nation? Where is the iron fist? Where is it, Mazooti Hamo asked himself, tugging at his hair like an enraged Jehovah? "Where is it?" Standing on the highest tower of the fort, he was invoking the power of Nayirian kings, as he leaned against the flagpole on which the Nayirian tricolor fluttered. "Where is it?" he kept repeating. But there was no answer. The somber, thousand-year ramparts stared blankly at Mazooti Hamo, at that last royal Nayirtsi, who was pulling at his hair while invoking the strength of Nayiri's past. But there was no strength; there was no response. And leaning against the flagpole on the top-most tower, Mazooti Hamo lamented bitterly and cried, as he had in that meeting, his tears scorching the thousand-year-old walls of the ancient fort. "No," he suddenly roared through his tears, rapping the flagpole with his hand. "It cannot be." He was shaken. His head snapped forward, like someone emerging suddenly from a coma. He wiped his eyes with his handkerchief. And he seemed to notice for the first time that standing around him were Comrade Varodian, the doctor, two Nayirian generals, and several officers. They were looking at Mazooti Hamo with reverence, silent and somber like the walls of the fort. "Where are they?" Mazooti Hamo thundered, his eyes glittering with rage. "Where are the others?" But "the others" Mazooti Hamo was talking about, like the will and strength he was conjuring earlier, no longer existed. A large number of officers had left the fort during the night, and had not come back. "And where is the garrison?" Mazooti Hamo went on, more quietly now, his voice strained. Comrade Varodian pointed with his finger. Mazooti Hamo looked in that direction and on the second tower of the fort saw a large troop of Nayirian soldiers, occupied at the moment in staring at him. "Forgive me," Mazooti Hamo pleaded, "but do they know how to fire cannons?" "Yes, they do," one of the generals assured him; and a childish, almost foolish smile brightened Mazooti Hamo's face. It was all finished, he realized; like the last flicker of a dying candle, the land of Nayiri flashed and subsided in his mind, wavered, darkened with soot, and expired. But no, he protested to himself, summoning what strength he had left, "it can't be." And he ordered that more soldiers be brought to the fort, more cannons emplaced, and where. Then he got into the car and returned to the city.

Surprising news awaited him there. A communique from the front revealed the heroic action of Nayirian soldiers who had pushed the enemy back ten miles, and had established commanding positions against them. There was more—the probability that they would soon resume the offensive and drive the enemy all the way to Erzerum. As Mazooti Hamo read the communique, he felt a wave of relief flood his heart. The doubt and despair that had seized him a short time before were suddenly wiped away, and he stood more determinedly, his shoulders, stooped with despair a little earlier, straightened now, his eyes clear and alert. A terrible fear had begun to grip the city. Those who had abandoned the outlying areas, and others from the upper quarter, had gathered all their belongings and were getting ready to flee. With thousands of others they had taken to the streets, and were heading for the station. The more prominent inhabitants of the city were already in the station, waiting to depart as others had done on earlier trains. What was happening in the station at that time was impossible to imagine. Thousands of desperate, frightened people were jammed together on the platform. Beside this utter chaos, the raising of the Tower of Babel, if indeed it ever happened, would have seemed a children's exercise. People were trampling and crawling over each other, trying to move forward in any possible way to get closer to the approaching train. Mothers were casting their children forward, over the heads of the mob, to enable them to get nearer, but the children were being smothered in the general uproar, and the women, unable to reach them, and pressed in from all sides, were themselves unable to breathe. Pregnant women were giving birth where they stood, and their screams were heard above the terrifying clamor of a mob gone mad. Men were fighting, women were scratching men's faces, and above everything else the snap and whine of the soldiers' whips. They were opening a path through the riot of confusion for various prominent Nayirian families who had passes issued by Comrade Varodian or Mazooti Hamo. But in spite of the special permits, it was not always possible to get them through. Like an enraged beast, the crowd surged in on them threatening to destroy both the soldiers and the prominent families they were escorting. Indescribable, unimaginable things were happening in the station, but what was happening in the city was even worse. Fires had started everywhere. When they left the city, the Nayirtsis, in their fervent patriotism, calmly set fire to their homes and shops, to keep them from falling into enemy hands. The local authorities might have opposed such feverish expressions of their sentiments if, as they say, they had but the brains to think with. But they had not, and the people did whatever their love of their county dictated.

But there was something even more astonishing. If the people were setting fire to their own homes and shops, who was it that set fire to the public buildings? Some claimed that the conflagration had started with them. The offices of "Light" were the first to go up in flames—can you picture that?—Mazooti Hamo's own office, which was temporarily closed, because in the first place there was no heating oil, and in the second place Mazooti Hamo had no time to spend there. The offices were burned down the day before Mazooti Hamo's return to the city, at night (he was already in the city the next morning). As soon as he learned about the fire, Mazooti Hamo ordered that the records and accounts of "Light" be recovered from the fire at all costs, though almost everything had already been reduced to ashes. So it was hardly possible. Then the small loan company building was ablaze. Then the police station. It was thus that the Nayirtsis, on fleeing the city, evinced their feverish love of Nayiri, spreading over all the streets the unique indelible expressions of the devotion—in fire and smoke. This was the state of the city when Mazooti Hamo received the encouraging communique.

He convened a special military meeting to institute drastic steps to stop the rout, to have the fires put out, to order the populace to remain where they were, to forbid flight from the city, and to terminate rail service. Mazooti Hamo personally ordered that the trains be detained in the station. He had Comrade Varodian dispatch an elite troop of soldiers to force the fleeing populace back to the city or, failing that, at least to prevent still others from joining them. At the same time he wanted to get the city council to reassert its authority and inspire a sense of security in the people; but almost all the councilmen had gone from the city. General Alosh was not there, nor was the shopkeeper Kolopotian, not Haji Onnik Effendi, nor any of the others. Only one remained, the representative of the upper district who had earlier demonstrated the depth of his political wisdom by seriously proposing that all the shops be smashed. You may recall what came of the proposal. Nothing. And what could Mazooti Hamo do with that one lone council member? Nothing at all. All he could do was shake his head and go home for a little rest. And that's what he decided to do. It was getting late anyway, and he was tired. There was a numb droning in his mind, the hum of exhaustion that seemed to be echoing the syllables of Nayiri. He had to get some sleep and, once in the car, he was about to order the driver to take him "home," when he suddenly realized that it was some time since his "home" had been in the city. Before leaving for the occupied areas, he had sent Ankine Parseghovna and the black-eyed prima donna away from the city, to free himself of family worries, since he was burdened enough with the concerns of Nayiri. Mazooti Hamo remembered his wife as he smiled wryly. He remembered Akribina Vladislavovna. "Drive to the fort," he told the driver and slumped deeper into the seat. Resting his head on his hands, he slept.

The next morning . . . it would have been better if it had never dawned. The light of that ill-fated day was barely visible when the people still left in the city, calm and reassured by the firm action of the military, and by the good news from the front, were shaken by the clattering of machine guns and the thunder of artillery, distant but drawing nearer. There was no power on earth, and none in heaven, that could keep them any longer in the city. Like a huge herd of cattle, tens of thousands, hundreds of thousands of them stampeded out of the city. One mass drove toward the station, another surged on to the highway. One after the other the city's houses lit up in flames. And in the smoke and fire of the abandoned homes, the Nayirian soldiers who had deserted at the front were scurrying about looting. From that moment the city could have been considered fallen. But the enemy had not yet closed off the escape routes; it was still possible to get away. No authority was left in the city. What leadership remained was gathered in the fort where military operations could be directed. Almost all the inhabitants of the city's lower district had left, and those of the upper district were leaving then; very few of the city's actual residents remained. In spite of that, it seemed full of all kinds of people, most of them peasants from the surrounding areas. There was no end to their number or variety. Among them was Telephone Seto who with uncharacteristic abandon had remained in the city until then. But now, with the help of his brother Kor Aroot and his life-long friend Enoch, he set fire to his popular cafe-restaurant, gathered up his whole family and made for the station. It took quite a while, of course, to manage all this; and by the time he was ready almost everybody else was gone. If we do not count the few who seemed determined to stay, Telephone Seto's group was the last to leave. Most of the others from his district had gone along the highway, but Telephone Seto elected to go toward the rail line, hoping that "with intervention from above," they would somehow manage to get on a train. And they succeeded; they all got on the train, though this impossibly good fortune materialized not so much because of "intervention from above," as by Telephone Seto's clever strategy. He went toward the tracks, not through the city, but along the road that went over the hill in the opposite direction, descending to the tracks some distance from the station. That's how they were able to get on the train. It was already midday, the sound of guns and cannon coming from less than two miles off, when Telephone Seto's group clambered down to the tracks. He led the way, his small child in his arms; hurrying behind him, carrying a large bundle, was his wife; then came Kor Aroot, a heavy pack on his shoulders, and Enoch. Having no other possessions, Enoch was carrying a scale he had made of old trays, a couple of weights, and some tea and sausages. It was in this manner that they reached the tracks, where they saw the train come to a stop before them, every car packed with fleeing Nayirtsis. The train had left the station and for some unknown reason had stopped there. Telephone Seto approached the train from the rear and came upon—by heavenly intervention, he was convinced—a wagon that seemed to have a little room. It was crowded, to be sure—"more than a thousand people," as Telephone Seto was to recount later—but at the back end Haji Manookov Effendi and the barber Vassil had a little space to spare. It appeared that they had terminated their procurement enterprise ("For whom were they to procure, when there was no army?"), and decided to join the exodus. "Let me have your child," Haji called to Seto, and Telephone Seto passed the child up to him. Then, with the help of the barber Vassil, they lifted Seto's wife aboard. There was no room for anyone else. "Go stand on the chains," Haji advised. They begged and pleaded and cursed, but finally went off and managed to mount the chains. They stood side by side, holding each other with one hand, and their belongings with the other. Just then the train moved. It was the last train out of the city. The enemy was apparently nearing the fort. Standing precariously on the chains, Telephone Seto, Kor Aroot, and Enoch—and in fact all the Nayirtsis in that wagon—stared in shocked disbelief at the fort. And when Kor Aroot shouted in astonishment, "Why don't our men fire back?", he was articulating everybody's thoughts. But sadly he would never receive an answer to his very proper question, not because no answer to it existed, but for the very mundane reason that, not two minutes later, Kor Aroot no longer existed. And not only him, but his old friend Enoch also. Hardly had he uttered his exhortation than the train suddenly jolted forward, shook violently, loosening Kor Aroot's grip on his pack. Then the train shuddered backward briefly. The pack went flying and instinctively Aroot reached out to retrieve it. But he missed, lost his balance and fell. "Ah . . . Aroot," Enoch called after him fearfully; he leaned toward his falling friend, stretching out his hand to grab him. He too lost his balance and fell. And in the next minute, rolling over the crushed bodies of those life-long friends, the last train from that Nayirian city was thundering away in terror. The enemy had already burst into the city where immediately there was death and ruin and massacre and horrors that cannot be described.

And thus, as the last train, rolling over the mutilated bodies of Kor Aroot and Enoch, left the Nayirian city, the enemy moved in to occupy it. We cannot relate what happened at that moment; that is beyond our competence. We will say only that many people were left in the city who were slaughtered by the enemy hordes. More critical than this was that Comrade Varodian, Sergei Kasparich, the doctor, and Mazooti Hamo remained behind along with all the others. They held their positions bravely until the very last minute, stayed in the fort and were taken prisoners. Some who were captured along with them, and by some miracle survived the massacre, later recounted how on the third day after the city was taken, the enemy by some cunning treachery delivered the leaders into the hands of the rabble troops who—can you picture this?—hanged Comrade Varodian, the doctor, Sergei Kasparich, and Mazooti Hamo himself, from those very telegraph poles which—incredible irony—had been erected two days earlier on orders from Comrade Varodian to hang deserters. The survivors described that wretched incident with enough detail to enable us to recount them here. It occurred roughly in this way. After they entered the fort, the enemy found Comrade Varodian, the doctor, and Mazooti Hamo on the highest tower, near the swaying flagpole on which the Nayirian tricolor flew. Noticing the grief of the Nayirian commanders, the enemy officers approached them with seeming respect, accorded them every courtesy, and took them to the city with appropriate ceremony. It is related that along the route, enemy officers honored them as they passed, and that the enemy commander in chief shook their hands and sought to ease their despair. Comrade Varodian, the doctor, and Mazooti Hamo were accorded such extraordinary attention by the enemy command; but two days later, in a crass betrayal, they were turned over to mobs of irregulars who beat them horribly and then hanged them. Comrade Varodian was hanged on the right, the doctor on the left, and in the middle between them Mazooti Hamo. And to compound the savagery, the mob nailed a board in the middle of the third pole, just above Mazooti Hamo's head, with the inscription—just picture it—in Nayirian letters:

M. H. K. N.

meaning: "Mazooti Hamo, King of Nayiri."

[1] Strabon and Ptolemy refer to the area of Kars by the name of Khorzin. The establishment of Kars is believed to have occurred in the 4th century. References to it in Armenian history begin in the middle of the 10th century, first as the seat of the Bagratid Dynasty, and then as the capital which was later transferred to Ani. Beginning in the 11th century, it fell to the Greeks, Georgians, Seljuks, Persians, and Turks. The Russians occupied it on November 6, 1877, making it a fortress in defense of the southern flank of the Russian Empire. After the occupation, the old city was enlarged, and a new city took shape.

[2] According to witnesses from Kars, General Alosh was the name most people gave to Alexander Tsitoghtsian, who had nothing to do with the military. The name Tsitoghtsian can be found in the weekly "Kars" as one who had contributed money on various occasions. He had several buildings in which state offices were located even before the war began. There was no five-story building in Kars, however.

[3] The famous fortress of Kars is on the right bank of the river. Earliest references to it date from the 10th century. Nerses Shnorhali gave the city the name of "unreachable castle."

[4] The construction of the Church of the Apostles began in 930 by the Bagratid king, Abbas I; it was completed in 942. It is one of the oldest monuments of Armenian architecture. In the 13th century the Turkish Sultan Murat III, transformed it into a mosque. It became a Russian church after 1879.

[5] A shrine southwest of Kars, about a mile from the city. Women who were unable to conceive went on pilgrimages to it.

[6] Also a shrine southwest of Kars, a cave near one of the ruined churches of the area. According to legend, a pious blind hermit lived there centuries ago. The place had become a picnic grounds in Charents' time.

[7] The flag of Czarist Russia.

[8] The reference is to General Vartan Mamigonian who led the battle against Mazdaist Persia on May 26, 451 in defense of Christianity. Vartan was killed in the battle along with 1036 of his soldiers. The Armenian Church has set the Thursday before Lent in their memory and the name day for all those who fell. Thus, anyone who does not have a saint's name, celebrates his name day then.

9 Reference is probably to the Rev. Hoosig who was one of the founders of the Committee of Dashnagtsootiun in Kars.

10 Charents refers symbolically to one of the early freedom fighters, Deacon Hagop of Moosh who, with S. Kookoonian and their friends, went to Kars in the 1890s. However, Kookoonian was arrested and after a few months in a Kars prison, was exiled to Siberia.

11 Charents alludes here to the Czarist persecution of Armenian national aspirations. Suppressed before the war, nationalism was encouraged by the Czarist regime when the war began because it accorded with its policy design.

12 According to historical records (Guerbeh), there had been a domed chapel in the southeastern part of the church, the floor had been covered with a stone arch and, according to legend, the remains of the son of the Armenian king Sempad, Abbas I, were buried there.

13 The exiles were usually political prisoners. One such was the principal of the Real School in Kars, Alexander Arkhipovich Yaroshenko from the Ukraine.

14 "Kindauer"—a dance resembling the Leskinga, danced by the "kindos"— the thieves and lower elements of Tiflis.

15 The national anthem of the Russian Empire (lyrics by V. Zhukovsky, music by A. Lvov.)

16 For a time in 1914, Hamazasp Nohradian-Mazooti Hamo had represented the oil company of the Nobel brothers in Kars. In 1915 he established his own company of petroleum products, calling it *Looys* (Light).

17 Reference is to General Andranik's visit to Kars on February 13, 1918. Two days later he left for Erzerum, on the eve of the recapture of that city from the Turks.